HUMANISM
AND
BEYOND

ROBERT L. JOHNSON

A PILGRIM PRESS BOOK
FROM
UNITED CHURCH PRESS
PHILADELPHIA

Excerpts from H. J. Blackham, Ronald Hepburn, and Kingsley
Martin are from the book *Objections to Humanism* by H. J.
Blackham. Copyright © 1965 by H. J. Blackham. Reprinted by
permission of J. B. Lippincott Company. Complete documen-
tation is given in Notes.

The scripture quotations are (unless otherwise indicated)
from the *Revised Standard Version of the Bible,* copyrighted
1946 and 1952 by the Division of Christian Education, National
Council of Churches, and are used by permission.

Library of Congress Cataloging in Publication Data

Johnson, Robert Lee, 1919–
  Humanism and beyond.
  "A Pilgrim Press book."
  Bibliography: p.
  1. Humanism. I. Title.
B821.J58   144   73–2817
ISBN 0–8298–0251–7

United Church Press
1505 Race Street
Philadelphia, Pennsylvania 19102

To the memory of my father and mother—
Delbert and Loretta Johnson

CONTENTS

FOREWORD

Humanism, in one or another of its many forms, is the only faith of millions in the contemporary scene. For this reason it must be taken seriously by all whose privilege it is to think about the questions which matter most. The ordinary humanist is a person who is convinced that intellectual honesty requires him to reject the supernatural, but who, at the same time, prizes some of the values which have emerged in the struggle of men to live nobly and well. Though the term Christian humanist is not a contradiction in terms, the combination is not commonly attempted, and the ordinary position is that in which men feel whatever wisdom they have comes from themselves, with no reference to any outside Source. It is this position which most requires examination, because its adequacy is far from self-evident.

We have had, in the recent past, many attempts to defend humanism in the sense of the autonomy of human values, and have also had some unqualified attacks upon it, but what we have lacked is the ability to appreciate without acceptance. This is exactly the field in which Professor Johnson exhibits genuine competence. While he is clear and unequivocal in his own theistic faith, he understands and appreciates what the nontheistic humanist is trying to support. He admires the humanist's rejection of a materialistic metaphysic.

Humanism, as Professor Johnson is well aware, is a word with a long history. At the time of the Renaissance the term was used to designate those who had discovered in themselves a remarkable affinity with the thinking of the classical writers of Greece and Rome. Turning their backs on the medieval world and its speculations, the characteristic humanists of the new age sought to model their own lives on the ideals which they found expressed in the greatest thinkers of the classical period. Some found they could honor the classical heritage and, at the same time, accept the Christian revelation, but, increasingly, and particularly in Germany, it was felt that one who concentrates on human values must reject the gospel. It is not uncommon, therefore, for thinkers who care greatly about man's improvement to assume without argument, that, since Kant, any attempt to anchor theism in rational inquiry is doomed to failure. Professor Johnson is a contemporary philosopher who knows that the intellectual situation is not that simple.

Central to all forms of humanism is emphasis upon the uniqueness of man. Man's life is seen to be different in kind from that of all other creatures, particularly the animals. The humanist glories, and rightly so, in the fact that man is a being who thinks, who can make decisions, who can alter his behavior by taking thought, who can make mistakes and can know that he makes mistakes, and, above all, one who can care. With Pascal, the modern humanist knows that, in spite of his finitude, he is more important than a star because he can know the star while the star cannot know him. There is a tendency, moreover, for the theme of human uniqueness to be carried farther, so that what is really affirmed is man's aloneness. It is conceivable that man is absolutely unique in the universe. In that case, man differs, intrinsically, not only from all animals, but also from all else. Then the principle of living is really "man for himself," with no support anywhere. The pathos of this situation, if it *is* the situation, is obvious. That such radical humanism, however, is the only option for an honest intellectual is far from obvious.

What pleases me now is that Robert Johnson has been able to devote his fine mind to a subject of such importance. I have observed his work as a teacher in Texas, Kansas, and now in Ohio, and I have admired his work. He combines, in a rare fashion, the clear head and the compassionate heart. I hope that his book will provide light on the pathway of all who are honest seekers and who can profit by his intellectual leadership. The book is directed to all who appreciate the values which humanism represents, but who are willing to go beyond it, if reason points them in that direction.

D. Elton Trueblood

PREFACE

Because of the "crisis of unbelief" in our day, there are many fugitives from the churches who are taking refuge in an old, yet quite modern faith, that of secular humanism. The purpose of this book is to examine the origins of this "faith," evaluate what appear to be its strengths and weaknesses, and then reexamine an alternative which some contemporary minds have already committed to the discard.

The growing popularity of secular humanism is due, in part, to the feeling of emptiness and futility which seems to characterize our age. Moved by the same secular temper more than a generation ago, Karl Jaspers wrote: "Beyond question there is a widespread conviction that human activities are unavailing; that our learning is of dubious worth; that existence is no more than an unceasing maelstrom of reciprocal deception and self-deception by ideologies."[1] There are others who have become disillusioned with traditional faiths and they tell us that the religious stage of history is now coming to an end and that man must assume responsibility for his world. He can no longer shift such responsibility to some religious power. But as Martin Marty has said: "An apparently godless age may be the best kind of time in which to 'do theology.' "[2]

It is true that the Christian is now forced to reexamine the substance of his creed. Yet despite waning faith and this picture of grim skepticism, he can never rest content with only a relative solution to his ultimate questions. Confronted with the uncertainties of his own life, man knows that unless he has a dimension that goes beyond his physical senses, he will never see beyond the physical environment. Putting it another way, Georgia Harkness tells us, "There is nothing to say to the secular world except to echo its own assertions unless one has a perspective from beyond it. Simply to reaffirm its assumptions and reinforce its values . . . is not a laudable service, but a pitiful surrender."[3]

But as we shall see, humanism has much to commend it and is worthy of a fair hearing. And even though I have approached this study with some bias, a sincere effort has been made to treat the competing views with the utmost respect. To use laudatory adjectives with reference to ourselves and give disparaging ones to those with whom we disagree tends to imply that our opponents are intellectually or morally retarded. No profitable study can proceed on such a basis.

Any critique should help one to become more aware of the multitude of optional positions. Not only is it possible to have many alternative selections of data, but it is also possible that the same selections of data may allow for conflicting interpretations. The arrogant voice continues to echo out of both the Christian and humanist camps—"You may have only what I clearly and distinctively perceive." But thoughtful men from both sides will probably concur with Lynn Hough, who has said, "It is a gracious thing that so many men live lives which are better than their theories, and have a logic for action which is more dependable than the logic of their thought."[4]

Some years ago Sabatier wrote: "The habit we have gotten into of putting all the truth on our side and all error on the side of others, of thus opposing light and darkness, not only falsifies the judgment; it sours the heart and poisons piety, it dries up the feeling of fraternity, and is the perpetual sign of individual and collective vanity." Though this study is approached from a theistic perspective, it is hoped that the attitudes just described will not be characteristic of the writing.

My indebtedness to those who have made earlier studies in this area will be apparent to the reader. However, the inspiration for this work has largely come from Elton Trueblood, one who has helped greatly to broaden my own religious and spiritual horizons, and who has enriched many lives through his ministry of encouragement. For reading the manuscript and offering helpful criticisms, I am grateful to Professor Higgs of the University of Michigan. To Professor William Orr of Centenary College I am most appreciative for his help in reading the proofs. Special thanks are also due to my wife, who has not only been a comfort and strength, but who also labored patiently in the typing of the manuscript.

1

HUMANISM: THE REAL RELIGION OF MODERN MAN

"It is meaningful . . . to make as many people as possible realize where they are; what they are missing; what has happened to them; what they have lost; why they are lonely, insecure, anxious, without ultimate purpose, without an ultimate concern, without a real self, and without a real world. Men are still able to feel that they have ceased to be men. And this feeling is the presupposition of all spiritual reconstruction."

—Paul Tillich[1]

Ours might be called the age of secular holiness. In some ways the secular saints seem to be outstripping the religious saints, for they are working with great diligence to improve man's lot and reduce the amount of suffering in the world. Enormous allocations are being made to alleviate poverty on local, national, and international levels. Many agencies of government find their budgets heavily weighted on the side of welfare and anti-poverty programs. High priority is given to those projects that bring direct relief to the poor and the disadvantaged.

These basic concerns extend beyond the immediate needs of food, clothing, and housing. Large sums are being raised and appropriated through community and government organizations for the improvement of public health. Some degree of medical assistance is virtually guaranteed to all who apply. Record amounts are being budgeted for research in a war with the most common diseases that afflict man. With a sizable percentage of our population moving into the upper age bracket, there is a new sensitivity to the problems of the elderly. Security for the aged, handicapped, and disabled is now accepted as an inherent right of the individual.

All of the elements of the environment over which man has some control are coming under the most careful scrutiny. Careless and willful contamination of air, water, and other resources essential to man's existence will soon cease, or come under the most rigid surveillance. The reclamation of land once ravaged by mining operations is now underway. Materials once regarded as waste are being recycled. Ecology is "in" from the college classroom to the kitchen sink.

Not only is there a genuine concern for man's physical needs, but his emotional problems and social relationships are now being studied in depth. There is a shift today away from the natural sciences to social studies. Social welfare, guidance, and counseling offices are found in every center of population. Man's behavior is being studied in a most careful and meticulous manner. For the questions keep recurring— Why isn't man happy? What does he lack? What is he trying to find? Any denial of man's freedoms comes under strong censure in both local and international situations. If evidence is found that man is being cheated, exploited, or abused, it is not long before such action comes under scathing rebuke, whether it be from minority groups, labor officials, or political factions.

All of the above concerns may suggest something to us— that this is not necessarily an irreligious age. Man has some very high priorities and commitments. He is not entirely selfish, nor is he indifferent to the sufferings of his fellow man.

Such attitudes reflect religious characteristics. Some presuppositions concerning value are implicit in the very nature of the projects. We see a type of religious activity to which many people are deeply committed. When we begin to question the character of this faith and the object of the commitment we discover that the real religion of modern man is humanism.

The religion of humanism has emerged from many contributing currents, social, political, and philosophical. In his Heidelberg lectures of 1848, Ludwig Feuerbach boldly announced that his aim was to convert "the friends of God into the friends of man, believers into thinkers, worshippers into workers, candidates for the other world into students of this world, Christians, who are on their own confession, half-animal and half-angel, into men—whole men."[2] We shall discuss the influence of Feuerbach and others in a later chapter, but for the moment we should recognize that these attitudes are characteristic of the modern secular temper.

Many of those who embrace humanism in its nontheistic form tend to hold that by believing in God one must surrender his autonomy, repudiate modern science and common sense, and drain off energy in worshiping God that should be used in ministering to man. It is also a popular idea today that to be enlightened means to be enlightened from religion.

Humanism is much more deeply entrenched in the Western world today than at the beginning of the century. It is seen in a variety of shapes and forms including atheistic, religious, social, and political expressions. Of the many kinds of religious and antireligious impulses and beliefs, the secular variety, with its rejection of traditional forms of faith and worship, has penetrated deeply into the popular consciousness. One modern writer contends that the world struggle today between Western democracy and Soviet communism "is polarized around a Eurasian and a Euro-American *secular* ideology, with no real religious ideological option available."[3] Many of us in the Christian tradition would like to think that Professor Marty is not entirely correct in this last observation.

One might wish that there were a real live tension between Christianity and this modern faith, but so far no serious conflict has erupted. This is what makes the situation so dangerous. All the players seem to be wearing white hats, and sometimes they appear to be halos. Both groups ostensibly are trying to promote human welfare, though there have been times when little more than lip service was given to this ideal.

Perhaps the surest way of drawing applause today is to extol the brotherhood of man. In practically all types of humanism one sees a disposition to be sensitive to the needs of others and to assert and defend intrinsic human values. Humanism is a belief in the nobility of man. There is an avowed concern for the health of the individual and society, although the profession of love, whether from the humanist or the Christian, is no evidence at all for its presence. Nevertheless, the challenge of humanism is not simply an intellectual one, but it is also a practical challenge. Whatever group does the most for the unfortunate and identifies itself with constructive social efforts will have a formidable argument for the other to answer.

But the appeal of this modern faith for "a good life in a good world" is not a quest that is unique to the humanist movement. This is an aspiration as old as the human race. The dress has changed to fit the age. Today it might be called the "Gospel of the Environment." This follows from the conviction that the best way to produce better men is to improve the climate and order in which they live. If we have better housing, this will mean better families. A more just economic order will mean better people. Actually, this "gospel" offers much that is desirable. But as Oscar Blackwelder notes, "Housing, justice, and freedom from fear give men at most the opportunity . . . to be better people. . . . There remains the age-old impossibility: unchanged men trying to change the world. . . . Social betterment strikes a mighty blow at the rim of life but not at the hub."[4]

When many of our young people go through their high school and college years with very little religious training they are often predisposed to some sort of secularism, even though they may have been initiated into some faith along the way. Possibly the outlook would have been different if they could have known the stimulus and challenge of real faith in God.

There are innumerable earnest men and women today who question the adequacy of science to furnish meaning or give guidance to life, but they also are finding no spiritual or intellectual satisfaction in the way religious faith is often presented. Many of these people may have repudiated an earlier faith because all they could see was creed without compassion, or "faith without works." Thousands of sincere, intelligent people are giving their lives to worthwhile humanitarian programs, working outside the pale and without the sanction of church or synagogue. We can only respect such people for living up to the highest that they know. If it is a secular humanism which they have embraced, perhaps they will reexamine some of their basic affirmations in the light of competing systems. In the same way the Christian, on occasion, needs to dust off some of his formulations so that he can still try to be "both intellectually honest and sincerely devout."[5]

There are certain attitudes and approaches in traditional religious life which deserve rebuke and criticism, whether it be superstition, hypocrisy, or self-righteous exclusiveness. There are few Christians who cherish these particular features that the humanists are rejecting. The positive values of humanism are already affirmed by most people. On the negative side, one must challenge the view that humanism tends to enrich life. It may be found that life is greatly impoverished through this secular world view.

As a humanist, H. J. Blackham is aware of the task confronting this modern faith. He says that without other help men must face together the common problems of mankind, the evils of ignorance, poverty and disease, insecurity, and other characteristic weaknesses of human beings. He states the case clearly: "Unlimited shared responsibility for creating the conditions for all of a life worthy to be called human, a human providence, is the colossal undertaking to be shouldered by man without God."[6] There are others along with Blackham who have not abandoned hope for a return to the "faith of their fathers," though they still think it is "a counsel of despair."

Perhaps modern humanists are more aware of the failings than of the merits of Christianity. A careful reading of history will show that the highest expressions of the Christian faith also reveal a hatred for tyranny and injustice. Every true Christian will earnestly contend for the worth and dignity of human life. He is persuaded, in fact, that many of the constructive efforts of humanism had their origin in the Judeo-Christian traditions. This point will be pursued in a later chapter. There is no disagreement between Christian and humanist about the fact that civilization must be improved.

We find the humanists contending that, as far as they know, man is the highest type of individual in existence. Whatever truths and realities are attainable by man must be sufficient for man. They maintain that if there is any worthy object of devotion, or any "real" god, it must be humanity considered in its highest and noblest capacities. There are some humanists who believe that the ultimate nature of things is eminently suited for the fulfillment of man's moral and religious powers. But the secular humanist does not concern himself with ultimate questions. He holds to the theory that since nothing is better known than man, then man should serve as the norm of thought and action. As this modern faith continues to shy away from metaphysical difficulties, there is the distinct possibility that it is erring on the side of oversimplification. If this is true, such a philosophy can never be a resting place for the one seeking a coherent account of all experience.

However, one cannot help but admire a certain nobility in the religion of humanism. Human beings using the resources of human minds, striving to comprehend a world of human experiences—this is an honest and straightforward ideal. We cannot be harsh toward anyone who accepts and appreciates the conditions of the natural world and "gladly gathers the perishable happiness that is to be had and enjoyed."[7]

But, in spite of all its admirable qualities and its appeal to certain noble characteristics of man, secular humanism keeps calling man to an eternal silence and meaninglessness. Because the humanist finds nothing in the universe greater than man, he denies that there is any evidence of cosmic purpose. But we believe that, sooner or later, the secular humanist will find that all of the facts of life cannot be included in the limited framework which he has constructed.

It is very possible that traditional religion has failed to keep its balance. God's transcendence has often been emphasized at the expense of man's basic responsibilities to himself and his world. Some forms of theistic faith may indeed lack relevance and, to the extent this is true, they deserve the rebuke and contempt of modern secular man.

While the Christian is doing some soul-searching the humanist also might reexamine the structure of his own "gospel" and the eternal meaninglessness which he has accepted. In the words of Michael Novak, "Perhaps no tribal myth in human history has emptied so many lives of substance as the American 'pursuit of happiness.' " He ventures the belief that "one of the most important developments of the '70's will be an exploration of the spirit."[8] And for the humanist who has taken a secular stance, Jacques Maritain has this word: "However generous an atheist may be, atheism turns to stone certain profound fibers of his substance."[9]

Ours may be an age in which the human spirit has lost contact with something mightier than itself. But if this is true, one need not despair. It has happened before, though perhaps not so many have shared such disillusionment. There were other ages when men chose to pursue nothing but the "facts" of the physical world. There were other days when men lost hold on commanding principles and were persuaded that all the forces of life could be explained by neat mechanical formulas. But as various theories become worn and discredited the human spirit probes again for a more satisfying answer to the perennial question of the meaning of life. "When all the goods of health, education, security, and wealth are distributed to him," says Novak, "[man] still hungers to know who he is."[10]

As our study develops we will see that theistic faith does not ask one to compromise his honesty or surrender his rational powers. But neither can God be relegated to the fiction of primitive desire. If there is to be belief in God, it can only come through fidelity to one's own conscience.

2

VARIETIES
OF HUMANISM

"Humanism is 'a ferment that has come to stay.' "
—William James

The word humanism is an ambiguous term. Ordinarily it has reference to the philosophical and literary movement which began in Italy in the last half of the fourteenth century and then spread into other countries of Europe, eventually becoming a significant factor of modern life. But the word also may refer to any philosophy which affirms the value and dignity of man and makes him the "measure of all things." It may have reference to any movement which takes human nature with its various interests and limitations as its theme. The term humanism has served as a kind of cover-all under which may be grouped men whose world views are neither primarily theological nor rationalistic. Humanism was at one time considered a halfway house between religious supernaturalism and scientific naturalism.

Today a humanist might be an educational reformer who believes that we now have too much of natural science and not enough of the humanities. He might be one who has a religious orientation and yet not hold to a personal God. One must go back many centuries to find the strands which have gone into the creation of this modern fabric.

PROTAGORAS AND HUMANISM
About the fifth century B.C. there was a group of men in

Athens known as Sophists. They were very doubtful about the possibility of knowing anything that was really true. A certain Sophist by the name of Protagoras was an agnostic. He set forth the dictum by which many humanists still chart their course—"Man is the measure of all things, of things that are that they are, and of things that are not that they are not." Protagoras wrote a book *On the Gods,* which he read in public. It began with the statement: "As to the gods, I have no means of knowing either that they exist or that they do not exist. For many are the obstacles that impede knowledge, both the obscurity of the question and the shortness of human life." For his views Protagoras was expelled from the city by the Athenians. His works were burned in the marketplace after they were collected from all who had copies in their possession.

An entire dialogue of Plato was devoted to Protagoras. In the dialogue, he has his teacher, Socrates, talking with Protagoras and several objections to the Sophists are raised. The question arose as to why people like Protagoras, who profess that they do not possess genuine knowledge, should presume at the same time to instruct people in worldly success. The students and the teachers at the same time might be doing the wrong thing, since they do not have any certain knowledge. It is not enough that one should be able to speak well, convince people, and be a leader. He should also know what to speak about, what to convince people of, and where to lead them. To Socrates, it is clear that the Sophists were "the blind leading the blind."

Diogenes Laertius, who wrote in the early part of the third century A.D., was not fond of Protagoras. He wrote his own epigram about him, concluding with this thought:

Protagoras . . . though
Thou 'scap'dst Athene,
Not so Hell below.

RENAISSANCE AND CHRISTIAN HUMANISM

The humanist movement proper began in Italy in the fourteenth century. Francesco Petrarch has been acclaimed as the first of the humanists. While he was devoted to the classics he had no use for paganism, except that the ancient culture served as a handmaid to Christianity. Petrarch never broke with the church of his day, though he was critical of some of its abuses.

A disciple of Petrarch was Giovanni Boccaccio. He too had a genuine reverence for ancient writings and he introduced new ideas about collating manuscripts. Boccaccio had a bitter hatred for the monks and considered them to be opponents of learning. He looked upon them as hypocritical pretenders to sanctity. By this time Florence had become the headquarters of the humanists, and the leader of the Florentine club of humanists was Luigi Marsiglio.

An attempt was made to turn many of the humanists away from Christianity to the mystical doctrines of Neoplatonism, but with little success. Marsilio Ficino insisted that Plato and Christ were colleagues, not rivals. With the sack of Rome in 1527, the Italian revival of learning came to an end, but the fire that was kindled in Italy had spread to other lands.

There was probably no humanist movement, as such, in France until around 1500, when the French kings became patrons of learning. This followed the closer relations between France and Italy. Joseph Scaliger and Isaac Casaubon were scholars who brought humanism to its highest level in France in the sixteenth century. The special work of Jacques Lefèvre will be noted at a later point.

In Germany such names as Johann Eck, opponent of Luther, Johann Reuchlin, and Philipp Melanchthon were to be associated with the humanist cause. Their influence will also be discussed further on.

Generally speaking, the early Renaissance humanists were scholars with a great love for learning and an appreciation of beauty, both of form and thought. They tended to reject medieval ideas and habits of mind, especially a decaying scholasticism. The humanists defended man's freedom to project his life in the world in an autonomous way. During the Middle Ages the empire, the church, and feudalism appeared as guardians of a cosmic order which man had to accept. The humanists worked to emancipate men and women from the restraints that custom and superstition had laid upon them.

But one must not oversimplify the movement. The Renaissance humanists were a small privileged group, with little interest in securing a wide audience. Some of them even "damned the printing press as the vulgarization of learning."[1] Being concerned with art and philosophy, artists and intellectuals were often contemptuous of the common herd. Yet there was a respect for talent and the insistence that man should enjoy his life in this world; views that have carried over into the democratic tradition.

In many ways the humanists of the Renaissance were conscious rebels. They rebelled against a way of life which they found to be corrupt, unlovely, and often untrue. They rebelled against a faith that had degenerated. But, as often happens, the rebel is not always certain of his directions. "The humanist," Brinton notes, "is a great rebel against medieval cosmology, but he has no very clear cosmology of his own. The humanist is a great individualist—he wants to be himself. But he is not very clear about what to make of himself."[2] Still, the humanists were in a sense opening a window and letting in some fresh air.

In the Renaissance period, technically speaking, a "humanist" was a teacher of the "humanities" which included the study of Greek and Latin, grammar, poetry, rhetoric, history, and moral philosophy. No doubt a large number of the classical humanists were nominal Christians who at least recognized that the church could serve a disciplinary function for those who had not attained a sufficient level of knowledge. Some humanists, veering away from conformity, cast off practically all authority. They became individualists. Not only was man the measure of all things but each man was a measure for himself. Such a view is characteristic of the modern temper.

The humanists introduced tools and standards of criticism. By a careful examination of its language, Lorenzo Valla was able to expose as a forgery the "Donation of Constantine." This document had been used by the popes to bolster the prestige of Rome and to establish control of the land around Rome later known as the "States of the Church."

Certain men of this period are known as "Christian humanists." The prince of all of them was Desiderius Erasmus, the illegitimate son of a Dutch priest and a physician's daughter.

He was born c. 1466-1469, became a priest in 1492, and entered an Augustinian monastery. Becoming disillusioned with the intolerance of certain dogmatic theologians and their resistance to modern methods, he left the monastery, became acquainted with the humanists, and made a trip to England in 1499. He became friends with John Colet and Thomas More. He had been impressed by Lorenzo Valla's critical method and exact philological exegesis. After much study and research, Erasmus produced, in 1516, a copy of the New Testament in Greek from manuscripts he could borrow. He became the foremost scholar in northern Europe. He made other trips to England, Rome, and Switzerland. At Cambridge he lectured on Greek. He is regarded by some as the first modern New Testament scholar, but he had a distaste for Hebrew. A prolific writer, Erasmus is well known for his *In Praise of Folly* and *Adages*, the latter being a collection of some three thousand proverbs. Erasmus was strongly antiwar and had deep concerns for freedom. Though he was called back to the monastery, he appealed to Leo X and was granted exemption by the Pope. Erasmus always submitted his judgments to the decisions of the church though he obviously differed on occasion. He made a strong attack against Luther in 1524. Before his death there was talk of making Erasmus a cardinal. Ironically, after his death he was branded as a heretic and some of his books were placed on the Index of Prohibited Books. Features of Christian humanism seen in Erasmus are his appreciation of the classics, scholarship, a passion for personal freedom, and an emphasis on the ethical nature of religion.

Out of that same period came Sir Thomas More and his *Utopia*. More was a close friend of Erasmus, whom he sincerely flattered by using proverbs and other materials from *Adages*. His acquaintance with *In Praise of Folly* is also quite evident in *Utopia*. As he envisioned well-adjusted men in a perfect society it is clear that More was dreaming of the triumph of humanism. In this nonexistent ideal state, one sees an attempt to reconcile classical Epicureanism and medieval Christianity. Pleasure is the end and goal of the Utopian communal state. But one also is impressed by the underlying appeal to justice, equity, and charity. *Utopia* not only had the approval of Christian scholars of the Renaissance and socialistic thinkers of the past two centuries, but it is viewed with favor by Communists of today. It is remarkable that a document should be revered so highly by both theists and atheists.

The chief representative of Christian humanism in France, and a contemporary of Erasmus, was Jacques Lefèvre, who was active mostly in and around Paris. He not only had an interest in the new Platonism of the day but he also had a broad acquaintance with mysticism, as well as the church fathers. His greatest satisfaction, however, came through his rediscovery of the Bible. He made translations and wrote commentaries on various epistles, as well as the four Gospels. He published French translations of the Vulgate versions of the New Testament and the Psalms. Though he never formally renounced Catholicism, he continued to hope for religious reform. His study of the Bible led him to a joy and satisfaction which he was able to impart to others. He came to the conclusion that man was not saved primarily through good works, but by love, and faith in the grace of God. Luther used commentaries of Lefèvre in preparing his early university lectures. One of Lefèvre's more famous disciples was Guillaume Farel, who was to become the fiery reformer of French-speaking Switzerland and the one who would constrain John Calvin to assist in the reformation that was underway in that country.

Christian humanism was represented in Germany especially by Johann Reuchlin, one of the most peace-loving and respected of the humanists. He was a theologian, lawyer, statesman, and educator. He was not only an excellent student of the Greek language but his knowledge of Hebrew was unsurpassed by any Christian scholar in Europe. It was his knowledge of the Hebrew writings that led him into one of the most bitter controversies of the day. There was a strong resentment of some Christians against the Jews, and a movement was afoot to have all Jewish books burned. The Emperor Maximilian consulted Reuchlin, who vigorously defended most all of the Jewish works including those on philosophy and science. After being cited to appear before the Court of Inquisition, Reuchlin appealed to Pope Leo X, who had the case remitted to another commission which exonerated him. The case was later reopened, Reuchlin's views were declared dangerous, and he was condemned to silence. The grandnephew of Reuchlin was Philipp Melanchthon, a superior scholar and friend of Erasmus, who was to be closely united with Luther in the years to come.

Christian humanism did much to prepare the way for the Reformation, though it was not identical with it, nor did it lead directly to it. A special contribution of the humanists was in the area of linguistic techniques. Through their publication of patristic literature and biblical texts they gained a knowledge of primitive Christianity which they could easily contrast with the church of their own day. Their criticism of many of the secular activities, as well as the immorality of the clergy, intensified the dissatisfaction of many Europeans with the church.

The Christian humanists also minimized the externals of religion, such as images, music, holy days, and the sacraments. Through the influence of Erasmus, Melanchthon cast doubt on the doctrine of transubstantiation, and Zwingli called for a more simple form of worship. Though Christian humanism was a predominantly intellectual movement, the emphasis was upon the inwardness of religion. The humanists tended to ignore Augustine's doctrine of original sin and stressed the fundamental goodness of man. They remained basically optimistic with respect to what might be achieved if Christianity could be studied in the light of the classics. However, this contrasted sharply with Luther's emphasis upon faith and Calvin's emphasis upon predestination.

NATURALISTIC HUMANISM

After Nicolaus Copernicus, contemporary of Erasmus, set forth his views regarding a heliocentric system, his observations were developed by Johannes Kepler and Galileo Galilei. It remained, however, for Sir Isaac Newton to show by mathematical demonstration that the motions of the heavenly bodies are explainable by gravitation. Though Newton himself was a deeply religious man, his findings were used by some as a means of disregarding Christianity. The physical universe no longer appeared to be a field responding to divine initiative but it was a realm of law to be interpreted in terms of strict mechanical cause and effect relationships. And so, men of science, philosophy, and literature began to project different moods into the popular thought patterns.

Francis Bacon has had both ardent friends and bitter enemies. He apparently was not a kindly man. He was ambitious for power and wealth. Yet he was immensely learned, versatile, and energetic, a true child of the humanist renaissance. Though his main interests were directed toward the natural world and the control of the forces of nature, he was not a materialist or an empiricist. While he insisted that sense and experience are the sources of our knowledge of the natural world, he also believed that faith and inspiration are the sources of one's knowledge of God and the supernatural. Though he saw the importance of the control of things, he is criticized for a lack of self-control in loyalty to moral standards. He believed that the achievements of science, when applied to every physical fact and relationship, could produce a world of comfort and everything necessary to the good life. "The modern world," says Lynn Hough, "has followed him almost to the abyss."[3]

While science was beginning to show men a new kind of heaven and earth, philosophy was beginning to challenge the claims of authority as set forth by religion. This was done in the name of reason. Seeking mathematical certainty, René Descartes, working his way back through a process of doubting objects and ideas, finally was convinced of the existence of God. He was sure that there must be a cause great enough and real enough to produce ideas in man, ideas greater than the "I" by itself could originate. But Descartes' assertion that all conceptions must be doubted until proved was to have a profound effect upon popular thought. Many who have followed Cartesian principles have ended up taking somewhat less than a Christian stance.

There were many writers and artists of the sixteenth and seventeenth centuries who were trying to find some way between traditional Christianity as it had been handed down and the new rationalism that was beginning to take all of the mystery out of the universe. The name of William Shakespeare obscures those of all other dramatists of Elizabethan England. He has been called an exuberant humanist. Shakespeare's genius was especially noted in his ability to present graphically to all men the elemental passions and drives of human nature. But in spite of his brilliance there is often a note of bitterness in his writing which is not characteristic of orthodox Christianity. We are not at all sure that Shakespeare was a Christian. He has no Christian warmth. To him, the world is an interesting, often exciting, but not a very sensible place for man. And he is not sure that there is anything man can do to change the scheme of things.

In the eighteenth century, Rousseau probably had more influence in shaping romanticism and later thought than any other man. He was the apostle of a movement away from artificial restraints. About Rousseau, Maritain writes, "What I call here absolute humanist theology is, above all, that of Jean Jacques Rousseau: the theology of natural goodness."[4] There was a surrender, with Rousseau, to undisciplined emotion. His key phrase, says Lynn Hough, might have been "Obey that impulse." But

> to be delivered from artificial restraint into the despotic power of lawless emotion is not much of a deliverance. The artificial restraints produce human sticks who call themselves men. The lawless emotions produce hectic and fevered animals who go through the world crushing everything in the name of impulses which are subjected to no standard above their own immense appetite. . . . Sensations take the place of judgment. Impulses take the place of the sanctions which are inherent in the intellectual and moral and spiritual life.[5]

The nineteenth century produced a number of men who gave strong support to the growing secular humanism. The French thinker, Auguste Comte (1798-1857), saw that science was giving man increasing powers to improve his environment but many social problems had arisen which menaced the well-being of society. The solution, Comte believed, was to create and develop a science of man. This he set about to do. Both sociology and positivism have derived from his efforts. He held that all genuine knowledge is knowledge that comes through the "positive" sciences. Because it is humanity that attains this knowledge, then reverence is due to humanity. He held that all speculation about the nature of ultimate reality is futile. To Comte, humanity is "the only true Great Being."

Following Saint-Simon and others, Comte held that there were three stages of intellectual development: the theological, the metaphysical, and the scientific. The study of society was in the third or scientific stage. After classifying the various sciences, Comte held that sociology was the completion of all the others. But there must be guidance in order to achieve sound social planning. The positivist social philosophy would be used to complete, clarify, and unite all the lesser and subordinate theories. Comte's ideal positivist society turned out to be a religious utopia. He called his new faith "the religion of humanity." It was an elaborate system of social ethics. The Great Being, or *humanity*, past, present, and future was to be worshiped instead of God. A positivist catechism was formulated and the priesthood was to be made up of secular sociologists. There were rituals, sacraments, and special festivals representing Order and Progress. Though women were excluded from public and political life they still had the responsibility of maintaining private morality. Marriage was indissoluble and widows could not remarry.

Comte's ideas were accepted in part by John Stuart Mill in England, and several of his assumptions have been embraced by twentieth-century logical positivists. Followers of Comte were particularly active in Brazil. A Positivist Church was established there in 1881. Also, on Brazil's national flag the words "Order and Progress" are found, indicative of Comte's abiding influence. Comte's philosophy and his "religion of humanity" have stimulated the rise of various secular religious movements.

Ludwig Feuerbach (1804-1872), ordinarily classified as a materialist or an atheist, at one time considered humanism as the most appropriate name for his philosophy. His famous dictum is "All theology is psychology." He repudiated the concept of divine transcendence and believed that man has his highest being in himself. He held that religion is merely the dream of the human spirit, the mirror of man's own nature and ideals. The gods can be nothing but products of a merely

been accused of driving God from heaven in order to help men to help themselves.[15] The theist has no serious problem with the relation between divine grace and human initiative. Instead of reacting to an imposed external power, the Christian believes that he is responding to a spiritual influence which tends to animate both his thought and conduct. He is convinced that the purpose of his life and his highest ideals have their roots in the ultimate nature of things. The theist does not argue with Dewey or any other humanist about the dignity and worth of human life. He is willing to acknowledge the tremendous gains that man has achieved through applied science. But the theist does not concede that science is capable of telling man the direction in which he *should* go. He is persuaded that values and ideals mean something in human life and these are the very intangibles that elude the methods of science.

Many other prominent humanists have emerged in the twentieth century, some kindly disposed toward religious ideals and others who have followed a purely naturalistic secular orientation. Roy W. Sellars, Max Carl Otto, A. E. Haydon, and Charles F. Potter have been strong advocates of humanist philosophy. Outside of religious and philosophical circles, writers like Joseph Wood Krutch and Walter Lippmann have made strong contributions to the ongoing influence of humanism.

Erich Fromm is widely respected for his efforts to restore more dignity to human life and to make men more aware of the dehumanizing tendencies of our society. He has helped many to gain a greater emotional and psychological stability. But Fromm's position is clearly humanistic. He writes:

There is only one solution to his [man's] problem: to face the truth, to acknowledge his fundamental aloneness and solitude in a universe indifferent to his fate, to recognize that there is no power transcending him which can solve his problem for him. . . . If he faces the truth without panic he will recognize that there is no meaning to life except the meaning man gives his life by the unfolding of his powers, by living productively.[16]

To Fromm, "Humanistic conscience is the reaction of our

total personality to its proper functioning or dysfunctioning."[17] In its humanistic sense, conscience is the voice of our true selves calling us to lead productive lives. Each person's conscience might be described as a mixture of authoritarian and humanistic elements. Fromm at times refers to his position as "normative humanism."

One can agree with Fromm that man must have a frame of reference from which he can derive an answer to the question of where he stands and what he ought to do. Man needs an emotional as well as an intellectual commitment. But the question remains, "Which frame of reference will it be, and to what will man commit himself?" There are competing ideologies—some theistic and some atheistic. Fromm says that man must decide with respect to (a) their truth, (b) the extent to which they unfold man's powers, and (c) the degree to which they answer man's need for meaning. Not everyone will agree that humanism is the basic value orientation which man should follow. To many, it certainly does not answer man's need for meaning. To the Christian, humanism, itself, needs the support of a belief in God if man is to achieve a sense of meaning in life.

Most humanists of this century have been quite specific and outspoken in affirming their philosophy. In the May-June 1933 issue of *The New Humanist* there appeared "A Humanist Manifesto," subscribed to and produced by more than thirty leading American humanists. It sets forth the views of men who call themselves *religious* humanists but it is readily seen that the term *religious* is not to be associated with any type of traditional faith that accepts the concept of the supernatural. Extensive quotations from the *Manifesto* are cited below so that the intent and affirmations of the document will not be in doubt.

> In order that religious humanism may be better understood we, the undersigned, desire to make certain affirmations which we believe the facts of our contemporary life demonstrate. . . .
>
> Today man's larger understanding of the universe, his scientific achievements, and his deeper appreciation of

brotherhood, have created a situation which requires a new statement of the means and purposes of religion. . . . We therefore affirm the following:

First: Religious humanists regard the universe as self-existing and not created.

Second: Humanism believes that man is a part of nature and that he has emerged as a result of a continuous process.

Third: Holding an organic view of life, humanists find that the traditional dualism of mind and body must be rejected.

Fourth: . . . that man's religious culture and civilization . . . are the product of a gradual development due to his interaction with his natural environment and with his social heritage. . . .

Fifth: . . . that the nature of the universe depicted by modern science makes unacceptable any supernatural or cosmic guarantees of human values. . . .

Sixth: . . . that the time has passed for theism, deism, modernism. . . .

Seventh: Religion consists of those actions, purposes, and experiences which are humanly significant. . . . It includes labor, art, science, philosophy, love, friendship, recreation—all that is in its degree expressive of intelligently satisfying human living. The distinction between the sacred and the secular can no longer be maintained.

Eighth: Religious humanism considers the complete realization of human personality to be the end of man's life and seeks its development in the here and now. . . .

Ninth: . . . the humanist finds his religious emotions expressed in a heightened sense of personal life and in a cooperative effort to promote social well-being.

Tenth: It follows that there will be no uniquely religious emotions and attitudes of the kind hitherto associated with the belief in the supernatural.

Eleventh: Man will learn to face the crises of life in terms of his knowledge of their naturalness and probability. . . . We assume that humanism will . . . discourage sentimental and unreal hopes and wishful thinking.

Twelfth: . . . religious humanists aim to foster the creative in man and to encourage achievements that add to the satisfactions of life.

Thirteenth: Religious humanism maintains that all associations and institutions exist for the fulfillment of human life.

Fourteenth: The humanists are firmly convinced that existing acquisitive and profit-motivated society has shown itself to be inadequate and that a radical change in methods, controls, and motives must be instituted. A socialized and cooperative economic order must be established to the end that the equitable distribution of the means of life be possible. The goal of humanism is a free and universal society in which people voluntarily and intelligently cooperate for the common good.

Fifteenth and last: We assert that humanism will:
(a) affirm life rather than deny it;

    (b) seek to elicit the possibilities of life, not flee from it; and

    (c) endeavor to establish the conditions of a satisfactory life for all, not merely for the few. . . .

So stand the theses of religious humanism. . . . Man is at last becoming aware that he alone is responsible for the realization of the world of his dreams, that he has within himself the power for its achievement.[18]

In more recent years, views similar to the above, but with an even more radical tone, have been espoused by Corliss Lamont in his *Philosophy of Humanism.* According to Lamont, naturalistic humanism considers all forms of the supernatural as myth. With no supernatural, Nature is everything and man is an integral part of nature. Placing ultimate faith in man this humanism believes that human beings possess the power or potentiality of solving their own problems through reliance upon reason and scientific method. In ethics and morality human values are grounded in this-earthly experiences and relationships. This secular humanism described by Lamont is the viewpoint that men have but one life to lead and they should make the most of it through creative work. He contends that "human happiness is its own justification and requires no sanction or support from supernatural sources."[19] Through the use of their own intelligence and by cooperating with one another human beings can build an enduring citadel of peace and beauty upon the earth. Such is the secular humanistic philosophy of Lamont, and his views are shared by many sincere contemporary men.

Other well-known humanists of the modern period include Julian Huxley, who states his position clearly in *Religion Without Revelation.* Charles Frankel shares much of Huxley's optimism in his book *The Case for Modern Man.* Humanists who are less optimistic, but who still cling to man's dignity and freedom, are such writers as Albert Camus, James Baldwin, and Samuel Beckett.

In very brief form we have attempted to sketch some of the varieties of humanism. There have been a number of man-centered theories of life in the course of human history. Some humanists have maintained their belief in the transcendent and supernatural. Others insist that ultimate faith must be placed in man, for man is essentially a part of nature and he can find no support outside of nature. It is this latter position which is contested in this study.

At a later point in the study we shall examine the materialistic assumptions, ideological presuppositions, and the value theory of naturalistic humanism. But perhaps first of all we should acknowledge the basic strengths of the humanist position.

3

THE STRENGTH
OF HUMANISM

"There are many men of good will for whom dogmatic and revealed religion has become impossible."

—Irving Babbitt[1]

It is clear that humanism is making many significant claims which must be considered. These claims are impressive. Humanists have enlisted the support of a broad spectrum of society. Educators, philosophers, and the common man have responded to the appeal. Many basic principles of the humanists are affirmed in the East and the West, by the weak and the strong.

In all fairness we should try to see in humanism an attempt of earnest spirits to reach the supreme values of which man is capable. Some humanists with rare ability have caught sight of levels higher than those on which the world is moving and they have made a lasting contribution to social betterment. Without doubt there have been times in the world's history when inhumanity fortified itself in institutions of trade, society, politics, and religion. In their efforts to restore a sense of the intrinsic worth of the individual, humanists have performed praiseworthy service.

As we look at certain aims of humanism we find that men with traditional religious backgrounds often share many of the same convictions. The humanist is deeply committed to the value of man as man, whoever and wherever he may be. The humanist affirms that man is equipped for and has the ability to utilize the forces of nature to improve and promote the well-being of himself and society. The humanist endeavors to make this a world of freedom, peace, brotherhood, and happiness. Practically all men of goodwill acknowledge that these are basic and essential goals.

One can only respect the mood of early Christian humanists who broke with the traditions and dogmatisms of the medieval period. They forged the tools and developed the techniques of scholarship. They inspired a love for learning and a renewed appreciation for the works of the great minds of the ancient world. They recognized that men of earlier centuries had reflected wisely and deeply on basic issues of life. Some of those early men had learned to live a good life while thinking of themselves both as rational beings and as creatures of the world of nature.

Christian humanists through their study of the classics discovered men who were interested in the rational life as a good in itself. In a day when practically all thought was controlled or mediated through the church, and the pace of secular activity was regulated by the feudal system, there was something deeply refreshing in this rediscovery of the world and of man. As the humanists challenged old ideas and accepted forms, they helped man to escape from the fetters in which human thought had been confined. Man found himself moving about in a wider, freer world where there was no restraining authority. This was a world where all facts were relevant and where the theories themselves were questioned or tested in the light of other knowledge. There was a new enthusiasm for poetry, art, and philosophy. Why should not man be as much interested in beauty as in righteousness? Either consciously or unconsciously, the humanists began to cultivate in their own lives the emphasis that God could be glorified through a better understanding of the gifts of his creation.

The humanists helped to inspire a growing appreciation for man as a free, independent, and concrete individual. They enlarged the sense of autonomy and self-sufficiency of man. They affirmed the things distinctively valuable and excellent in man. This independent spirit produced a great wave of creative activity which was expressed in a variety of ways, educational, economic, and political. Such activity was a stimulus for a general cultural rebirth.

Humanists stressed the role of intelligence in sifting man's ideals. They learned the joy and exhilaration that comes through an understanding of facts. They became enemies of all unreason. As his knowledge increased, man had learned to use his skills to control natural forces for human ends. Through their impressive results the humanists added a new dimension to the physical comfort and well-being of man. Whether or not it was their intention, the humanists brought a proud and creative spirit to the world. Following the early Greeks the humanists applied a clear and fearless intellect to every domain of life.

One cannot help admiring the men who contributed to such notable advances in scholarship, literature, art, and the sciences. Most of the early humanists were men with deep religious convictions who did much to advance biblical knowledge and Christian ideals. The names of John Colet, Thomas More, Philipp Melanchthon, and Desiderius Erasmus are remembered with great respect. The humanism of the Renaissance had a very definite religious bias. In the school operated by John Colet, one finds the following statute: "My intent is by this school specially to increase knowledge, and worshipping of God and Our Lord Jesus Christ, and good Christian life and manners."[2]

As humanism evolved from the sixteenth and seventeenth centuries, quite different attitudes arose toward religion. Today, both religious and secular humanists refuse to accept blindly the presuppositions of any religion or authority. And for this they should be commended. It is admirable for any thinker to challenge the postulates and validity of time-worn traditions and customs and subject them to intense examination. One of the common failings of man is to hold opinions and judgments which are clouded by his own personal, or inherited, prejudice.

Humanists are quite right in asking whether the human mind can know that its perceptions really grasp the external world. It is true that whatever may be the ultimate eludes present apprehension. And it is quite natural that one should

have reservations about the goodness of the ultimate processes of the world. The final good is still beyond man's earthly
reach.

Through the years, humanists have challenged a number
of base and unworthy fears which have been found in certain
expressions of religion. They have sought to expose the
superstition, empty forms, obscurantism, and "double-talk"
which are sometimes found in religious faith. Some humanists
believe that religion, with its eschatological hopes, tends to
obscure the concrete business of living in this world. In the
modern day, humanists have been outspoken in their criticism
of many churches for their indifference to social problems.
Certainly, many of the traditional forms of Christian thought
have not significantly improved the attitudes of many church
people.

Many humanists criticize traditional religion because they
believe it largely represents a flight from reason. They believe
that institutionalized faith suffers from many abuses—its dog-
matism and intellectual narrowness; its aspiring to a false
certitude; its ecclesiasticism, intolerance, and persecution,
and playing on superstitious fear. It may be true, as Huxley
suggests, "Selfish preoccupation with personal salvation has
been the curse of many religions."[3] A further view is that
religion, in seeking some intellectual explanation, has invented
an ad hoc explanation, which may be satisfactory enough as a
provisional hypothesis, but which has mistakenly been set up
as immutable truth.

The humanist proudly affirms that his "faith" requires

no shrinking before the supernatural; it invents no god
made in the image of his worshipers; it does not pretend to
explain the unexplainable. It promises no paradise; it
threatens no hell. Fixing attention on this life, its aim is to
promote happiness here and now by spreading among all
people friendliness, helpfulness, and mutual trust.[4]

The humanist must be respected for his beneficent skepticism. He makes it a matter of principle not to affirm what he
does not know. It is wrong, he believes, to go beyond evidence
no matter how comforting the conclusion might be. To the

humanist, "Belief in the supernatural seems like a leap in the dark which opens the door to all sorts of vagaries and superstitions."[5] It is the better part of wisdom, he believes, to avoid questions pertaining to ultimate ends because they are usually not productive and they often terminate in only vague and obscure understanding. For this reason the humanist can live for the day, or possibly for tomorrow, restrict his curiosity and be content to take life as it comes and death when it comes.[6] The humanist is convinced that "humanism offers more by which men can effectively be true to themselves than does religion."[7]

Those humanists favoring democracy for its recognition of man as an end in himself naturally favor those political, economic, and social structures which are more conducive to the best personal development possible for the greatest number. They are openly critical of every attempt to gain special privileges by any sectarian group or interest.

American humanists proudly claim that they can find justification for many of their humanist principles from the life and labors of Thomas Jefferson. They point to the Declaration of Independence, which affirms that all men are equal in their unalienable rights to life, liberty, and the pursuit of happiness, and that governments are only means and servants to secure these rights. In this light, humanism is looked upon as the faith of democracy. The emphasis upon man as the creator of his own fate is seen to be in line with democratic evolution.

The emphasis that the humanist places upon science and objective truth must be recognized. The following "Creed of Science" evokes the respect of almost every right-minded person:

> To love justice, to long for the right, to love mercy, to pity the suffering, to assist the weak, to forget wrongs and remember benefits—to love the truth, to be sincere, to utter honest words, to love liberty, to wage relentless war against slavery in all its forms, to love wife and child and friend, to make a happy home, to love the beautiful in art, in nature, to cultivate the mind, to be familiar with the mighty thoughts that genius has expressed, the noble deeds of all the world, to cultivate courage and cheerfulness, to make others

happy, to fill life with the splendor of generous acts, the warmth of loving words, to discard error, to destroy prejudice, to receive new truths with gladness, to cultivate hope, to see the calm beyond the storm, the dawn beyond the night, to do the best that can be done and then to be resigned—this is the religion of reason, the creed of science. This satisfies the heart and brain.[8]

Many humanists are optimistic in their faith that men have the intelligence and skill to build security in a free and just world. They believe that men of good will can meet the challenge of privation, hunger, and disease. They point to many instances of man's dignity and courage, and his willingness to sacrifice himself for others, as can be seen in the dedication of so many men of science.

The humanists should be commended for their reaffirmation of basic human values. They endorse the supreme worth of human personality. They acknowledge no master race, but stress the equality of man. They have been enemies of tyranny and advocates of freedom. They believe that men should be permitted to make responsible choices in life, and this is another reason why they tend to favor democratic processes of government. Especially in a free society, humanists are anxious to point out alleged abuses to the working man because of certain defects of the free-enterprise system.

Besides many in the Judeo-Christian faith, there were a number of humanists in Europe who set themselves against the inhumanity of totalitarianism. Some resisted the Nazi movement to the death on grounds of a humanistic faith in rational justice and humanitarian idealism.

It is commendable that humanists are often in the forefront in promoting programs dealing with human and social welfare. They speak out for specific, concrete, and positive social action. Like humanitarianism, humanism lends support to those groups and organizations that render immediate and active service to men. They see no reason for delay when man has present needs that must be attended to.

Humanists are optimistic about the betterment of society and the kind of world in which man might someday live. They have been able to communicate at least a secular sense of human solidarity. Without question, millions of people who either knowingly or passively embrace a secular world view are finding a reasonable, if not exciting, fulfillment in daily living. Not only are human intellectual achievements deeply gratifying, but other activities bring great satisfaction as well. Most humanists are convinced that "this is the good life." Julian Huxley states his convictions, "I believe first and foremost that life is not merely worth living, but intensely precious: and that the supreme object of life is to live; or if you like to turn it around, that the great object of living is to attain more life—more in quality as well as quantity."[9] Huxley states further, "I believe that the whole duty of man can be summed up in the words: more life, for your neighbor as for yourself. And I believe that man, though not without perplexity, effort, and pain, can fulfill this duty and gradually achieve his destiny. . . . I believe in the religion of life."[10]

According to Erich Fromm, a highly respected contemporary humanist, the crucial question is whether man "lives love and thinks truth. If he does so the belief systems he uses will be secondary. If he does not they are of no importance."[11] Commenting on *Socialist Humanism*, edited by Fromm, Professor Schilling makes this observation:

> Fromm's position makes unmistakably clear the essential characteristics which all scientific and philosophical humanists, whether religious or secular, have in common—a fundamental belief in the oneness, improvability, and ethical-social responsibility of man, coupled with a conviction that the fulfillment of his possibilities depends on man's own efforts.[12]

Although we shall have much to say further on about the differences between the Christian faith and humanism, there is a sense in which the Christian faith has an important ally in the humanistic ideals of our civilization. The Christian must always appreciate any movement which helps to promote the values and ideals that lead to human communities of law, art, science, and a just society.

It is hard to be critical of these positions of the humanist. Even the nonhumanist will affirm that the aims and ideals which we have just noted are most worthy.

But our special concern has to do with the secular type of humanism which has revived the earlier emphasis of Protagoras that "man is the measure of all things." Whether one calls himself a humanist or not, when this position is taken, then the corollary doctrine will follow, that nature is the complete and inclusive scene of human affairs. It is *this* "religion," *this* variety of humanism, which we feel must be challenged, and a discussion of its limitations follows.

4

THE INADEQUACY
OF HUMANISM

"To propose to man only the human is to betray man and to wish his misfortune, because by the principal part of him, which is the spirit, man is called to better than a purely human life."

—Aristotle

Our objections to humanism are not to its highest forms and ideals but rather to its avowed or implied limitations. The greatest weaknesses are not in the context of its achievements but in its exclusions. To the extent that modern man is following the religion of humanism, he will have to learn with the men of all past generations that the mere plenitude of life will never satisfy the most urgent cries of the human heart. It is one thing to tell man that he is free, autonomous, and self-sufficient, but it is another thing to insist that man can supply his deepest needs through his own resources. Humanism has no power to purge from man his greed, covetousness, and selfishness in his pursuit of and possession of this world's goods.

When humanism began to assume a secular stance it exposed itself to the same criticisms as all other secular philosophies. Humanism is especially vulnerable at several points. How adequate is naturalism as a world view? How can one structure an adequate value theory on the basis of naturalistic philosophy? Can one fully portray the nature of man by viewing him only from the horizontal dimension? Do the disciplines of modern science provide an adequate frame of reference for modern man to achieve his highest aspirations? Has the humanist borrowed his *good* from his religious ancestors? These are questions that warrant our special attention as we try to evaluate this modern faith.

NATURALISM AS A WORLD VIEW

There is a certain simplicity about naturalism which makes it attractive as a world view. Every day man has contact with this *real* world of the senses. Because he can verify his experiences through sight and sound and touch, he is duly impressed with the permanence and stability of the natural world. Why introduce perplexing and difficult theories of the universe when naturalism is the clearest and most obvious explanation?

Before subscribing to the above position one should examine the logic of a purely naturalistic world view. We admire the candor of certain humanists who have been willing to do this. In his essay "A Free Man's Worship," Bertrand Russell looks at the problem. He admits that ultimately there is nothing for the nontheistic humanist to look forward to but "the trampling march of unconscious power," and "the slow, sure doom" which falls "on him and all his race, . . . pitiless and dark." Russell continues with the same deep pessimism in these further lines:

> That man is the product of causes which had no prevision of the end they were achieving; that his origin, his growth, his hopes and fears, his loves and his beliefs, are but the outcome of accidental collocations of atoms; that no fire, no heroism, no intensity of thought and feeling, can preserve an individual life beyond the grave; that all the labor of the ages, all the devotion, all the inspiration, all the noonday brightness of human genius, are destined to extinction in the vast death of the solar system, and that the whole temple of Man's achievement must inevitably be buried beneath the debris of a universe in ruins—all these things, if not quite beyond dispute, are yet so nearly certain, that no philosophy which rejects them can hope to stand. Only within the scaffolding of these truths, only on the firm foun-

dation of unyielding despair, can the soul's habitation henceforth be safely built.[1]

Writing as a humanist, H. J. Blackham has pointed out that humanism might be called an exercise in vital subtraction: God goes, the soul goes, sin and death remain; the outlook becomes extremely bleak.

Sharing the same mood as Russell, another humanist, Professor Max Otto, wrote these lines in his *Things and Ideals*:

It is thus a constructive social suggestion that we endeavor to give up, as the basis of our desire to win a satisfactory life, the quest for the companionship with a being behind or within the fleeting aspect of nature; that we assume the universe to be indifferent toward the human venture that means everything to us; that we acknowledge ourselves to be adrift in infinite space on our little earth, the sole custodians of our ideals.[2]

In the above quotations, both Russell and Otto have confessed that to them, there is no purpose in human history or in the world. When asked to account for the existence of an ongoing world, Russell can only say "the world is simply there and is inexplicable." When he contends that there is no ultimate reason for the world he doesn't arrive at this through reason or logical analysis. Here we encounter a most serious inadequacy of secular humanism. Why should we trust the reason of one who is claiming that the world is ultimately irrational? Why should the skeptic be permitted to maintain that reason is on his side? The humanist affirms cause throughout the natural order, but he hastens to deny cause when it represents a principle that would explain the finite universe. An ongoing universe does not explain itself. The only possible explanation is that there is a sufficient cause, which in and of itself, brought the world into existence. This cannot be demonstrated, but it is not irrational.

The humanist presents his case on the basis of reason and then confesses that ultimately the world is irrational. How rational is humanism? Is it not irrational to suppose that purely sterile, unguided, unconscious matter could produce scientists, saints, and philosophers? And one does not solve the problem by the use of the word "emergent."

As M. Izoulet once stated, "We cannot base a terrestrial optimism on cosmic pessimism." There are difficulties in conventional theism, but the same difficulties will not be resolved by the humanist who ignores the problems of metaphysics. One may respect the humanist for not wanting to venture beyond empirical borders, but the humanist must be reminded that belief in the eternity of matter is a gratuitous assumption; it is a *belief.* Some humanists see the weakness of their position at this point. Dr. Corliss Lamont, a humanist, admits that "humanism stands in need of a sound metaphysics."[3] But another humanist, Professor Nowell Smith, disagrees. He says, "It is not too much to say that such a metaphysics would be the death of humanism."[4] Martin Marty has said, "The outstanding original feature of thoughtful and radical unbelief in our time is its reluctance to deal with transcendence."[5] The humanist finds it most difficult affirming reason on the one hand and yet having to affirm on the other hand that the world is ultimately irrational.

THE PROBLEM OF VALUES

If there is no God and ultimately no purpose for the world, then human history has no other purpose than the purpose it chooses to assign to itself. And if there is no God, no ultimate Being, then obviously there can be no absolute or ultimate values.

Some contemporary humanists acknowledge that their philosophy is most vulnerable at the point of value theory. In a volume which he edited, the British humanist H. J. Blackham had this to say, "Life as the end of life, . . . experience for its own sake, the finality and sufficiency of human values, this is the citadel of the humanist position. Is it defensible?"[6] Another humanist writing in the same volume reflects upon the problem with a similar note of skepticism. He asks how one should view man's domination of the planet and his uniqueness as a thinking, choosing, self-determining being. He answers that one may view it with exhilaration or with a sense of bleak loneliness "as an affirmer of values in a realm where value is otherwise unknown."[7]

This points up the fact that there is a great deal of moral ambiguity and uncertainty in secular humanism. Where men no longer believe in a God with an overruling moral purpose they will inevitably decide that they must create their own moral and value structures. Every human code must necessarily be arbitrary and relative for there remains no universal principle by which human codes can be judged for better or worse.

Humanism, according to Lamont, believes in an ethics or morality that grounds all human values in this-earthly experiences and relationships. It holds as its highest goal the this-worldly happiness, freedom and progress—economic, cultural and ethical—of all mankind.[8] Sartre, agreeing with Nietzsche, says that man is himself the creator of his values. It is man who confers meaning and significance upon the experiences which he has in and of the world.

It is not difficult to trace the sources of the ethical and moral theory found in humanism. In the days of Plato, the Sophists maintained that all truth is relative. Though this concept has not gone unchallenged it has been transmitted from age to age and it is still an integral part of humanistic value theory. In the last century John Stuart Mill held that it is not possible for man to discover ultimate ends and purposes, therefore he should strive for that good which produces the greatest amount of happiness for the greatest number of people. John Dewey believed also that man should not concentrate upon ideals which he could not achieve. Man should forget about ultimate ends. There are no fixed goals or ends for man but only specific ends-in-view. Dewey recognized no highest good or supreme test of value except social growth.

The ethical theory of Bertrand Russell is highly subjective and is sometimes known as *emotivism*. Russell had some serious reservations about his own ethical theory but he still did not hesitate to affirm: "It is we who create value and our desires which confer value. In this realm we are kings, and we debase our kingship if we bow down to Nature. It is for us to determine the good life, not for Nature—not even for Nature personified as God."[9]

Russell's ethical theory has come under sharp attack from such men as G. E. Moore, George Santayana, and Edgar

Brightman. While Russell argued ethics are strictly subjective he found himself introducing objective arguments against what he considered to be social or political evils. He held to the premise that a man ought to satisfy his desires but still claimed that there is no certainty of ethical knowledge. His basic premise became tautological—the satisfaction of desire is good because it is good to satisfy desires. Russell often expressed ethical judgments with great vehemence but he still ruled out the possibility of ethical knowledge. A normal answer to his critics was "I feel such desires, so why not express them?"[10] He was nevertheless aware of his logical incompatibility. He says:

> I am accused of inconsistency, perhaps justly, because although I hold ultimate ethical valuations to be subjective, I nevertheless allow myself emphatic opinions on ethical questions. If there is any inconsistency, it is one that I cannot get rid of without insincerity.[11]

The very fact that Russell refuses to be insincere is indicative of moral concern and implies that he is persuaded of the existence of moral value. Again he states: "I am not prepared to forego my right to feel and express ethical passions; no amount of logic, even though it be my own, will persuade me that I ought to do so."[12] When he speaks of his *right* to express himself on moral issues, it is clear that he is not persuaded of his ethical skepticism. The concept of *moral right* is at variance with both positivistic and humanistic value theory. Showing that he still is not entirely happy with his own position Russell observes, "While my own opinions as to ethics do not satisfy me, other people's satisfy me still less."[13]

Both Russell and A. J. Ayer have much in common, though perhaps Ayer is the more radical of the two. The views of both men could be classified as ethical skepticism though Ayer would lean more toward a purely emotive theory of value. To Ayer, ethics are nonexistent and ethical judgments have no validity. From his stance as a positivist, ethics can be given a place only among the pseudosciences. It is an illegitimate study.

As one looks at the implications of such a position he finds it completely illogical. All acts of cruelty and violence and the suffering and death of innocent persons would have no moral significance. Any malicious falsehood to enhance one's position at the expense of another would not be reprehensible. One might make noises to express his feelings but this would only be emoting. If this theory should be accepted then the nerve of moral endeavor would be destroyed along with the moral foundations upon which society has been built. Complete ethical skepticism is finally self-defeating and self-contradictory. How can one say that his position is right or good, or true, better or best, if it is not possible to evaluate or criticize the views or experiences of someone else? The very fact that he prefers his point of view and would like others to recognize it is an admission that he has found some basis for value judgment.

Whether we admit it or not, we are continually making value judgments. It is part of our very nature to do so. Perhaps there are not many humanists who would go to the extreme position of ethical skepticism such as that of Ayer or Russell, but the secular humanist is hardly a handbreadth away with his moral relativism. He still affirms values in a realm where value is otherwise unknown.

Numerous other writers of the twentieth century have held to varying degrees of ethical and moral relativism. Edward Westermarck held the view that ethics are based on emotional reactions in which there is a basic impulse to repay the good or evil that has been done to oneself. What one calls good is that which arouses in him the emotion of approval. Whatever arouses in one the emotion of disapproval is considered bad. Émile Durkheim stressed more the role of society in forming one's moral standards. The feelings of approval or disapproval which characterize good or bad conduct are determined by the opinions of society. William Graham Sumner held that moral values are merely the folkways of a given society. The good is only a reflection of the prevailing customs of present society. Karl Mannheim expressed similar views. He maintained that all our ways of thinking are ideologies. Even the concepts of good and right are purely ideological. All moral values and norms are relative. An absolute standard is unobtainable.

We see that many writers have contributed to the relativistic climate in this century. But what does this relativism in morals imply? If all values are relative then do all values become equally arbitrary and irrational?

Though truth and value are not necessarily synonymous terms, there can be no radical separation between them, and neither can be understood apart from the other. Every naturalistic philosophy occupies an ambiguous position regarding the question as to whether there are tests of truth in the realm of value. There is always the matter of the testing of values themselves. The truth about a value is no less important than any other truth.

As John Baillie has said: "I can do good consciously and rationally only if I believe in the good and in its objective independent significance in the world." He states further:

> Naturalism has never yet succeeded in making it credible to us that our values can continue to live and breathe when they have been robbed of their ancestral faith in their own cosmic significance. We can do without the reward, perhaps we can do without the spur and without the crutch, but we cannot do without the assurance that the struggle in which we are engaged is a real fight and a fight that counts. To renounce that faith is no true heroism, but only foolish heroics and a selling of our most sacred birthright.[14]

As Blackham and other humanists take a second look at their philosophy they become aware of some serious limitations of their position. They know that if there is no cosmic purpose then human beings are reduced to the helplessness of achieving nothing higher than awareness of their own futility. The path they have taken makes them question whether this temporal order of human existence provides anything more than an absolute frustration of human purposes and aspirations.

Humanists have relied heavily upon science to give them guidance in their ambitious programs for mankind. But some of them have enough candor to admit the inadequacy of the method which they have chosen. Julian Huxley writes: "Science . . . confronts us with a basic and universal mystery—

the mystery of existence in general, and . . . of mind in particular. Why does the world exist? Why is the world stuff what it is? . . . We do not know."[15] As he pursues the matter Huxley makes some most interesting observations. He says that this world can present itself as "alien and even hostile to human aspiration" yet we must learn to accept it as "the one basic mystery," to see it as furnishing a "background of reverence and awe" and fostering a "sense of wonder, strangeness and challenge."[16] The question is immediately raised as to why anyone should revere the unknowable. If it is wrong to revere in theism, why not in humanism? Contending with Huxley at this point, Ronald Hepburn, himself a humanist, says, "The humanist lacks an adequate or appropriate object of reverence and awe, still more an object of numinous awe."[17]

In the Hibbert Lectures of 1929, S. Radhakrishnan took issue with humanistic philosophy and his reasoning is still persuasive. He said: "Life is a great gift, and we have to bring to it a great mood; only humanism does not induce it." He was equally clear in the following observations:

The prophets of disillusion call upon us to seek truth, create beauty and achieve goodness. We cannot strive for these ideals if we are convinced that we are unimportant accidents in a universe which is indifferent, if not hostile to them. If the nature of the world is malign, our duty is to defy. It is only fair to ask where the urge to do these noble things comes from. If the strivings after truth, goodness, and beauty are a part of the cosmic plan, then it is not unfriendly to us.[18]

Even Bertrand Russell made quite a concession when he said:

It is a strange mystery that nature, omnipotent but blind, in the revolution of her secular hurryings through the abysses of space has brought forth at last a child, subject to her power, but gifted with sight and knowledge of good and evil, with the capacity of judging all the works of his unthinking mother.[19]

Whether a person is a humanist or a theist one has adopted some moral and metaphysical stance. He has selected a particular world view and certain concepts of value in preference to others. Elton Trueblood helps us to see the matter in clear perspective. He says:

> If we hold a philosophy which denies the existence of objective truth we necessarily cut the nerve of moral effort, since there is no use in disciplining our minds for participation in a meaningless endeavor. . . . Though the truth is something which we cannot grasp with perfection, much of our glory lies in the fact that we can make approximations to it.[20]

The humanist argument of relativity which says that all of our ideas of truth and value have arrived by a process of growth, is by no means persuasive. One can argue with equal force "that our ideas may become *closer* and *closer approximations* to objective truths and values which we do not make but discover."[21]

If there is no absolute value or ultimate truth then there should be considerable freedom for each man to choose his own life style. But it is recognized that along with free choice there is responsibility for the choice made. Some choices might work to the disadvantage of other men. Can there be no guidelines for human behavior? Are not some modes of conduct to be preferred over others? It seems as though one should be able to give good reasons for choosing his particular goals rather than others which he might have chosen. Many humanists hold that "agreement is the ultimate criterion for values as well as for facts."[22] This is often a popular and helpful solution but it may also be disastrous. Blackham is cautious in his critique at this point. "There is," he says, "no supreme exemplar of humanist ethics, because, on humanist assumptions, there is no summum bonum, no chief end of all action . . . no teleology, no definitive human nature even."[23] As a humanist he contends that there are "many patterns of good living, which can be exemplified, and none that is best or comprehensively or exhaustively good."[24] He admits that relativist principles can work evil as well as absolutist ones, but he believes by considering all relevant matters and through the systematic appeal to experience that any one-sidedness can be corrected.

On the other hand the theist would argue that values are more than creations of the human mind. They are not merely empirical accidents. There are values which reveal to man an order of being which is more than human. They are suggestive of a spiritual reality which gives significance to what happens in the temporal process. The theist believes that there is a transcending purpose that is cooperating with him in his quest for ideals. He is convinced that human life points beyond the contingent to a world of another dimension. If the humanist should ever admit the ultimateness of values he would at the same time acknowledge the existence of a spiritual factor in the universe.

As a humanist, Ronald Hepburn is very candid as he looks at the difficulties of his position. He says:

> What we [humanists] look for here but fail to find are ways of resolving the ambiguities, of guiding and controlling our interpretations. The traditional faiths do provide such controls—at least for the most important choices of attitude. Both grandeur and misery may characterize man on a Christian view: yet the doctrine of Creation and redemption steer the believer from the extremes of Promethean pride or a total villifying of man. It is only with the help of such doctrinal controls that stable, wholehearted and clearcut religious attitudes are maintained. In Christianity the chief of these are attitudes *to God* and his purposes. . . . This stability and wholeheartedness are [religiously] important. Their absence is debilitating. To revere—but only to a point; to marvel—but only to such and such an extent; to wonder—from this viewpoint, but to be bored or horrified from the other; these ambiguities seem inevitable in any humanist religious outlook.[25]

"If this be so," Hepburn says, "it injects a measure of irony into humanist claims to be the 'emancipators of religion.'

Religion was to be delivered from such 'encumbrances' as the supernatural . . . but freed also from the controls that gave direction and stability to its attitudes and evaluations."[26]

To be sure, there are difficulties in the theistic position, but they are hardly more difficult than those faced by the humanist as he sets forth his value theory. We are told by the humanist that it doesn't matter what the ultimate nature of reality may be if only we are prepared to do the proper thing. But we cannot be sure what is true, or whether anything is true at all. But still, he says, life is something that is certain and definite, and so we should occupy ourselves with the improvement of life. "Devotion to values," says S. Radhakrishnan, "would be inexplicable, if men were entirely products of nature."[27]

There is always the problem as to whether man's life and his mind really participate in objective, significant structures or whether life and mind are merely the expression and prolongation of interests. This is a vital question for any theory of value. And we find that humanist value theory rests upon a faith principle no less than any other system in which men seek to find meaning in the world.

The central faith of the humanist is the self-sufficiency of man. Values are strictly relative and contingent, and yet the humanist asks man to dedicate himself to that which has no ultimate meaning. If the humanist accepts the supreme worth of personality on faith, without scientific criticism, why should *this belief* be superior in any way to that of the theist? When the humanist insists on the *ultimacy* of this value then it would appear that his position is rooted in a reality which is deeper and more comprehensive than that which he ostensibly claims. Furthermore the humanist has certain *beliefs* about education, economics, democracy, and social relations that would either promote or retard his basic theories. We find that there are a number of assumptions having no empirical support that are implicit in the humanist position.

Granting the right of the humanist to state his beliefs, this does not necessarily mean that such beliefs are more convincing than other views. If man is only a part of nature and nature is neutral or indifferent to the human venture, why should man have any special concern or compassion toward fellow human beings? As a theist one may believe that God's power makes possible the conservation of highest values and that ultimate values are eternally realized in Him. But the humanist can only see a blind force operating without concern for the creature which has been produced. He asks us to believe that there is a process, devoid of purpose, which has produced an intelligent self-conscious being who searches for truth, beauty, and goodness. But this *product* of the neutral process is not acting in an indifferent manner. He is aspiring to goals and purposes which transcend a purely naturalistic order.

A. E. Taylor writes:

What confronts us in actual life is neither facts without value nor values attached to no facts, but fact revealing value, and dependent, for the wealth of its content, on its character as thus revelatory, and values which are realities and not arbitrary fancies, precisely because they are embedded in fact and give it its meaning.[28]

According to secular humanism, death would mean permanent and complete annihilation. If this should be true, says Alan Richardson,

Does not our whole being cry out and rebel against the irrationality and meaninglessness of man's quest for value? . . . can one contemplate with equanimity the prospect of the extinction of all values, when finally the life of man on this planet—however far hence the end may be—is brought to a close by the operation of ruthless natural forces? "That value itself should perish," said A. S. Pringle-Pattison, "that is the one intolerable conclusion."[29]

Does humanism include, preserve, and fulfill all human values? Life may be more than humanism has declared. It cannot be less. For it is quite possible that man *is* related to a Reality beyond the natural order.

THE NATURE OF MAN

We face conflicting views as to what man is, what he ought to be and do. One cannot demonstrate by scientific description and analysis that one view is correct and that others are wrong. From early days man was described by the Orphics as a "child of earth and of starry heaven." Aristotle observed that man has the same five senses and the same biological appetites as other animals. But in addition to these, man is able to reason logically, set up tentative goals, and develop social and political systems to achieve these goals. Pascal saw man both in his greatness and in his misery, in his exalted state and also in his wretchedness.

Man thinks and acts. He discovers and interprets. He has been discovering things since his earliest days on this planet. He is still in the process of discovering himself. Man's knowledge of things and his remarkable ability to put these things into intricate relationships have enabled him also to escape from the earth at least for limited periods of time. When only distorted images can be seen, man even tries to escape from himself.

All that we have come to know about this complex creature through the natural and the social sciences and through religion and art—as reflected in various cultures—influence our conception of man. "It is possible," said Rufus Jones, "to read human life at many different levels. We can read it up or we can read it down. We have been passing through a period of stark naturalism, and the humanism that has emerged from this naturalism is windowless above."[30] Whether a person is a humanist or a theist, only when he comes to some conclusion as to what man is will he then commit himself to those ideals and values which appear to have the greater degree of relevance and truth.

The practical issues of life are decided largely not only by what we think of man but also by *how* we think of man. Men's lives are shaped by the power of ideas, especially ideas concerning human nature. One need only think of Marx, Nietzsche, or Freud, and what a deep influence their ideas have had upon the political and social life of modern man. Marx viewed man as being determined by economic forces; Nietzsche saw man driven by the will to power; whereas Freud held that man is primarily motivated by his deep-seated sexual instinct.

A materialistic view of man has emerged as a result of an

There must be at least as much to learn about the inmost character of the real from the fact that our actual spiritual life is controlled by such-and-such conceptions of good and right, such-and-such hopes and fears, as there is to learn from the fact that the laws of motion are what they are, or that the course of biological development in our planet has followed the lines it has followed. It may be that this is a grave understatement.[41]

The naturalistic humanist may fail to see that he is a victim of a world of mathematical uniformity. The air-tight system of impersonal laws, beyond which there is no reality, could well be the creation of his own mind. As Martin Marty again has stated, "The outstanding original feature of thoughtful and radical unbelief in our time is its reluctance to deal with 'transcendence.' "[42] There is a general unwillingness in all forms of naturalism to accept the reality of a transcendent order, one which is beyond our immediate experience.

Charles West, in his *The Power to Be Human,* says that "Christians must help demythologize science and technology. Science and technology are neither means of salvation nor demonic powers, but neither are they neutral. They belong within a human political and ethical context where they must be mastered for the service of man."[43] When it comes to the problem of human relations in time of trouble the teaching of scientific certitude is not the most satisfying prescription.

The humanists are frequently guilty of ambiguity especially as they use the terms "nature" and "science." Is nature always to be equated with matter-in-motion, and is naturalism to be identified with materialism? There are some naturalists who include within nature mind and its values as basic entities. Sometimes nature is spoken of as simply that which science studies. At other times it is regarded as the object of any kind of rational inquiry. Nature is spoken of as reality, and in this sense all reality can be known by scientific method.

Also when one uses the term science, does one mean that the social sciences are scientific in the same sense as the natural sciences? Are there other valid ways of knowing besides the scientific method? These points are open to serious question as the humanist presents his naturalistic world view.

A BORROWED GOOD

Our final criticism of humanism is not necessarily the least important. In an earlier chapter we noted that humanists are earnestly striving to improve the well-being of man and society. They are endeavoring to make this a world of freedom, peace, and brotherhood. Nearly all men affirm the positive values of humanism. The quest for "a good life in a good world" is not peculiar to the humanist movement. Men of past ages formulated noble concepts of human relations. The Egyptians, Babylonians, Chinese, and other cultures developed commendable standards of social conduct. But we see especially in the Hebrew and Christian writings exalted claims for justice, mercy, and right dealings among men. It is the substance of many of these claims that we see incorporated in humanist concepts of social justice. Humanists have borrowed some of their finer principles of justice and fair dealing from the very theism which they are trying to oust. The good which they have borrowed from others they have made no better.

We are not contending that the biblical ideal was achieved in Old or New Testament times any more than our social ideals are realized today. But we are saying that human and social virtues were no small part of the biblical faith. The Bible speaks of an ideal heavenly kingdom, a kingdom not of this world, but this community has its beginnings now, among men. In both Old and New Testaments, justice and mercy are stressed more than creeds and ceremonies. One serves and glorifies God more through service and sacrifice for human beings than through ritual or the chanting of praises. The social order is to be characterized by justice, good will, and consideration for needy mankind.

It is not difficult to document these claims. Most of the prophets were champions of social justice. Amos was an outspoken critic of the church people of his day who were ethically corrupt. He cried out against those "who oppress the poor, who crush the needy (4:1)," and others who had "[sold] the righteous for silver, and the needy for a pair of shoes (2:6)." Others were charged with "[afflicting] the just," taking bribes, and turning aside "the poor in the gate from their right (5:12, KJV)." As a spokesman for the Lord, Amos issued the fervent plea "But let justice roll down like waters, and righteousness like an everflowing stream (5:24)." The prophet had nothing but scorn for the feasts, fasts, and the rituals that were being substituted for human compassion and true worship.

Micah was a country preacher who faced men exact in their outward performance of ceremonial requirements, but who were sadly deficient in their concept of justice. He said that there was something more noble than burnt offerings and sacrifices. "He has showed you, O man, what is good; and what does the Lord require of you but to do justice, and to love kindness, and to walk humbly with your God (6:8)."

Isaiah urged the men of his day to have deeper concerns for suffering humanity. He pleaded that they might "learn to do good; seek justice, correct oppression; defend the fatherless, plead for the widow (1:17)." He protested against the greed, selfishness, and falsehood which had become so common.

The message of Hosea is similar to that of the other prophets—"I desire steadfast love and not sacrifice, the knowledge of God, rather than burnt offerings (6:6)." It is clear that the prophets understood that the will of God implied justice and mercy to one's fellowman. True religion was conceived in terms of character. Piety that was divorced from social morality would fail to achieve God's purposes.

The book of Deuteronomy contains one of the greatest pieces of humanitarian legislation of all time. The social ideals and ethical principles by which men were to live are clearly outlined in this remarkable code. Both economic and political justice are woven into the very fabric of religious life. There is awareness in the code that human well-being depends in great measure on economic conditions. One finds legislation to prevent the exploitation of the poor and underprivileged. An employer was to give the manual laborer his hire at the end of the day. And every seventh day the laborer was entitled to rest from his labor.

Because poverty always contributed to human distress there were laws which aimed at removing the basic causes of poverty. Originally the land was parceled out so that each family was given the opportunity to make a living. Property that was signed over as a pledge or security was to be released back to the owner after a legally specified time. If one's coat were given as a pledge it was to be returned to the poor man before nightfall so he could use it for warmth.

Yet in spite of preventive legislation there was often poverty. As always, there were widows and orphans. Illness and accidents often resulted in distress. Hunger was alleviated to a great extent through special laws that gave the poor certain rights to glean in a neighbor's field or vineyard.

Efforts were made to secure justice for all men—the poor, the rich, the citizen, and the alien. Judges were to deal impartially regardless of the status of the individual. Bribery was condemned and listed as one of the most serious crimes. False witnesses were to suffer severe punishment.

It is perfectly clear that just and righteous dealings between men as well as economic and social justice were vital concerns of the religion of the Old Testament. Many of these laws also formed a basis for New Testament teachings. Yet in spite of the noble provisions of the law to encourage justice and equity in human relations, the intent of the law was circumvented in countless ways. Ceremonialism and a faithful mechanical performance of the letter of the law were often substituted for the higher ethical practices.

No prophet ever spoke more vehemently than Jesus as he rebuked the hypocritical practices of priests, scribes, and Pharisees. In substance, his mission was to remove man's alienation from God and to assure man of the Father's love, mercy, and forgiveness. But at the same time his teachings and his ministry bear out his own estimation of the supreme value of human life. No other great teacher placed such a high value on the individual person. Jesus challenged every practice that tended to sacrifice man in the interest of things. He taught that "The sabbath was made for man, not man for the sabbath (Mark 2:27)." He expressed contempt for orthodox religious people who would show no compassion for a needy human being.

In his ministry as well as in his teachings Jesus showed intense concern for both the physical and mental well-being of man. In his desire for men to have abundant life there is evidence that Jesus was speaking of the whole man, both his physical and spiritual nature. The prayer for daily bread was no less a petition for minimal economic security. The laborer was deserving of his wage for he too must be able to secure the material necessities of life. Jesus warned against those who would call upon his name and yet neglect to feed the hungry.

The tests of the New Testament by which men stand or fall are exceedingly practical. The judgment scene as depicted by Jesus in Matthew has to do with questions of helpfulness and unselfishness. The same emphasis is found in the book of James. "If a brother or sister is ill-clad and in lack of daily food, and one of you says to them, 'Go in peace, be warmed and filled,' without giving them the things needed for the body, what does it profit? (Jas. 2:15-16)" Any business or economic policy, or any social relationship which is indifferent to the consequences of such a policy or relationship on human lives is in itself a repudiation of the teachings of Jesus.

Though recognized as a great religious teacher who helped men gain a clearer perspective of God, Jesus also insisted that duty to God and duty to man are inseparable. The first and great commandment to love God was joined directly to the requirement that man was to love his neighbor as himself, whether that *neighbor* might be a stranger, foreigner, or even an enemy. The love of Jesus extended to all men without distinction of class or race. He loved both the poor and the well-to-do, though their problems were dissimilar. He prayed for those who were responsible for his crucifixion. His love extended beyond the barriers of misunderstanding, mistrust, and hatred—attitudes that so often set man against man and nation against nation. Jesus finally gave his own life in the interest of a cause greater than any individual life. Through his magnanimity and supreme devotion to the right he taught that it is not just life itself but it is the good life that has value. To him, man is a being of infinite worth.

In the early Christian community, whether they were masters or slaves, lettered or unlettered, men were regarded and treated as brothers. This spirit of brotherhood was one of the factors which helped to demonstrate that the members of this fellowship were more upright than their pagan neighbors.

The social concerns of the early Christians were apparent from the beginning. We are told that by the year 250 A.D., there were some fifteen hundred dependents, widows and orphans being cared for by the church in Rome.[44] Financial help was given to those who were unemployed while efforts were made to find employment for them. The church provided for the families of those who were imprisoned or exiled for their faith. When there were famines or pestilences, relief offerings were sent to the unfortunate. This social ministry among the needy served to commend the faith as much as any element of doctrine.

There was no legislation that required the sharing of one's goods with another but many times property was sold and the proceeds were donated for common use whenever special needs arose. The early Christians had no intention of imposing a new economic structure on society. With but few exceptions they possessed a fraternal spirit which they had learned from One, who himself had given his life in service to others. Though the faith was God-centered, it was also humanitarian.

We have sketched these references from the Bible in order to make it perfectly clear that biblical faith is replete with humanitarian and social concerns. In fact, the evidence is quite strong that the respect for human dignity and justice found in humanism did not originate with that philosophy. Maritain is convinced that "Western humanism has religious and transcendent sources without which it is incomprehensible to itself," and these sources "are both classical and Christian."[45] Speaking of various contemporary forms of Western humanism, Maritain says:

It is easy to see that, if there still remains in them some common conception of human dignity, of liberty and of disinterested values, this is a heritage of ideas and sentiments once Christian but today little loved. . . . Is it not a sign of the confusion of ideas reaching throughout the world today, to see these formerly Christian energies helping to exalt precisely the propaganda of cultural conceptions opposed head-on to Christianity? It is high time for Christians to bring things back to truth, reintegrating in the fullness of their original source those hopes for justice and those nostalgias for communion . . . which are themselves misdirected, thus awaking a cultural and temporal force of

Christian inspiration able to act on history and to be a support to men.[46]

Though the humanists have a strong social orientation it seems clear that many of their ideals originated in an earlier religious context. The good they have we can only commend, but we should not credit the humanists with any unique role in promoting justice, human dignity, and the well-being of man.

5

THE TRANSCENDENCE
OF HUMANISM

"If we would maintain the value of our highest beliefs and emotions, we must find for them a congruous origin. Beauty must be more than an accident. The source of morality must be moral. The source of knowledge must be rational. . . . A lofty form of Theism becomes, as I think, inevitable."

—Arthur J. (Lord) Balfour[1]

In 1953, twenty years after the publication and signing of the "Humanist Manifesto," those of the original signers who were still living were asked to express their reactions to how the Manifesto had stood the test of time and what changes, if any, should be considered if a new statement were prepared.[2] Other responses were solicited from contemporary humanists. There was considerable support for the original document but it is interesting to note that there were also some serious reservations about the validity of the statement. An original signer, John H. Dietrich of Berkeley, had this to say:

I think you are wise to let it [Manifesto] stand as an historical document. It is definitely a dated instrument and represents what I have come to feel is a dated philosophy —a philosophy too narrow in its conception of great cosmic schemes, about which we know so little, and concerning which we should be less dogmatic and arrogant. It in no wise reflects the humility which becomes the real seeker after truth. But that is the kind of fellows we were in those days. In fact, I was one of the chief offenders, and I confess it now in all humility. I see now that my utter reliance upon science and reason and my contempt for any intuitive insights and intangible values, which are the very essence of art and religion, was a great mistake. I think the Humanism of that period served a good purpose as a protest movement, but its day is passed. What I am trying to say is that the positive side of Humanism was and is fine—its insistence upon the enrichment of life in its every form; but its negative side, cutting itself off from cosmic relationship, and denying or ignoring every influence outside of humanity itself, I think, was and is very shortsighted.[3]

These observations are quite revealing. Dietrich has mentioned especially the inadequacy of humanism in its narrow conception of great cosmic schemes and its tendency to cut itself off from all cosmic relationships. He notes that it is a mistake to deny or ignore intangible values and influences that may lie outside of humanity itself. Another original signer of the Manifesto, Jacob J. Weinstein, of Chicago, gave this reappraisal of the position he had taken twenty years earlier:

Humanism is essentially a young man's faith. It is Promethean and therefore limited. How long can you shout defiance at the heavens? Life's slow strain finds it inadequate in situations of emotional stress. There are mysteries which cannot tolerate an agnostic answer. There are moments when the refusal to call upon the Friend behind phenomena leads to paralysis of the will. To accept only what the intellect clears makes for a glacial astringency of the blood. To refuse to personalize "the power not ourselves making for righteousness" leads to a sense of rootlessness and makes it almost impossible to communicate one's faith in moral integrity to his children. To accept the mytho-poetry of the classical religions does indeed open the door to superstitions and irrational binges of the emotions, but it is a chance we must take. Better to take it than close the door on the tides of inspiration that bring us the profound and sustaining insights.[4]

It is especially in regard to these observations and the limitations noted in the previous chapter that we feel it is necessary to explore and reexamine a world view that transcends the basic naturalism of much humanistic philosophy.

It is probably true that effective belief in God does not rest on argumentation and is never produced by it. "No man," says A. E. Taylor, "has ever been led to a living faith in God simply by a chain of syllogisms. Indeed, I doubt whether *any* conviction which has seriously changed men's lives and conduct has ever been a matter of mere cold 'intellectualistic' assent."[5] We must agree, too, with Balfour, who says that metaphysics does not appeal, and has never appealed, to the world at large.

> For one man who climbs to his chosen point of view by a metaphysical pathway, a thousand use some other road; and if we ask ourselves how many persons there are at this moment in existence whose views of the universe have been consciously modified by the great metaphysical systems . . . we must admit that the number is insignificant.[6]

But Balfour also notes:

> There are for all men moments when the need for some general point of view becomes insistent; when neither labour, nor care, nor pleasure, nor idleness, nor habit will stop a man from asking how he is to regard the universe of reality, how he is to think of it as a whole, how he is to think of his own relation to it.[7]

Our purpose in this chapter is not to "demonstrate" the being of God, for this cannot be done. Neither can we create faith where it is simply nonexistent, as Taylor says, for only God himself can do that. But we hope to project the view that it may be unbelief (not belief) which is the unreasonable attitude. If natural science does not represent the whole field of knowledge, then "the silence of natural science . . . about God," writes Taylor, "is no reason for denying that God may exist."[8] When we ask whether God exists or not, it is the question as to whether the whole course of events in which the man of science discovers uniformities of sequence is or is not guided by a supreme intelligence to the production of an intrinsically good result.[9]

Those who accept secular humanism as the religion of modern man find all their value and all their hope in what humanity can do for itself. Their primary assumption is that the universe taken as a whole is nonteleological, i.e., it does not show evidence of design. Some humanists regard the world as only the outcome of chance combinations of basic physical units whose random movements or impacts have built up the extremely complex but wholly natural order that we know. It would be difficult to disprove this account of the universe with flawless logic, but the theoretical probability of such an occurrence is so remote that it commands little or no respect.

Beyond this random, fortuitous, and highly improbable theory of the origin of the natural world, many humanists prefer to speak of *natural law* as an explanation of what has come about. Robert Calhoun helps us to see the inadequacy of this view.

> This suggestion may mean that natural law is a controlling factor which exerts constraint upon moving units, and makes them go this way rather than that. But the physical sciences know nothing of law in this sense. It is in fact a hybrid conception which seeks to read into the physical world such constraint as statute law may put upon human behavior, but at the same time leaves out both legislator and policeman and treats the law as somehow self-made and self-enforcing.[10]

This is certainly as much a fabrication of reality as any other that has been devised by man.

A somewhat different, yet related world view is the suggestion that the universe is guided by some unconscious but quasi-purposive force. Schopenhauer used the term will to designate this power. Bergson called it the "élan vital," while Marx and Engels preferred the name "dialectic." To call the process *dialectic* is merely to rename it, and to rename it with a term directly related to mental activity or behavior. As Calhoun notes, it is strange when one will suggest that the behavior of the universe is essentially like that of mind, but at the same time deny that mind is present.

We must respect the integrity of any man whose total thought and experience do not lead him to believe in a personal God. One should not attempt to make him feel guilty for his disbelief when this is an act of integrity on his part. But at the same time it is often difficult to see any special merit in the reasoning he uses to arrive at seemingly incredible explanations of the universe. The humanist or atheist does not escape belief by disbelieving in God. He is still ordering his life on the basis of some faith principle with regard to ultimate creative factors in the universe, or lack of them.

Our task now is to examine a concept of the world which to many appears to be more adequate than what is seen in humanism or any other philosophy.

A THEISTIC PERSPECTIVE

Before examining particular arguments in support of a theistic world view, one should acknowledge certain limitations which are apparent in most any type of rational inquiry. First of all, it is easy to imagine that one is seeking objective truth when all that one really wants is some confirmation of a faith which one is too lazy to scrutinize. Furthermore, one can't always take the purity of one's own motives for granted. We are often motivated by pride or desire for security or conformity. There is the danger also that when we try to define religious faith in strictly logical terms we may be cutting the ground from beneath ourselves. For logic cannot deal with the ineffable and it is often the ineffable that is the source of vitality in religion. If one could resolve the question of God's existence it would not be done on one level of experience alone.

Another difficulty of a purely rational approach is that all thinking moves on assumptions. This is true for the theist, atheist, or humanist. So one must exercise special care about the number and kind of assumptions he makes. Neither theistic assumptions nor atheistic assumptions are proofs but they deserve a careful examination by inquiring minds. Rational arguments may help to make the notion of God intelligible and they often remove some of the intellectual barriers that stand in the way of faith. Whitehead suggested that "no reason can be given for the nature of God because that nature is the ground of rationality."[11] John Baillie reminds us that "next to the foolishness of denying God, certainly the greatest is that of proving Him."[12] The greatest issues of philosophy and religion are not susceptible to empirical proof or demonstration. It is usually the case that when one's interest is mainly rational his search will end in speculative uncertainty.

Finally, there is no other study which demands such a many-sided wisdom as the attempt to describe, explain, or interpret the meaning of God. Even before the biblical era men were seeking to define the ultimate, and philosophers and theologians have ever since examined and debated the evidences. A generation ago Bishop Francis McConnell wrote: "The most barren of all quests would be a search for something absolutely brand new to say about God, or for God, or against God. There is almost nothing new to be said today either for theism or atheism—excepting in phrasing or emphasis."[13] Being fully aware of all the above limitations, there is still need for a reexamination of certain theistic affirmations. As Roger Hazelton has said, "Rational, argumentative knowledge of God is certainly not the only kind there is; it may not even be the best kind. Yet it may well be necessary on occasion."[14] Compared with certain humanistic and atheistic views, most theistic convictions appear to be quite reasonable. There will be occasion later on to make reference to revelation, but for the present we shall consider those aspects of theism which lend themselves to a more objective investigation.

The theistic hypothesis. We shall be looking at a number of general statements and definitions of theism by various writers, but one of the most articulate of contemporary scholars has given us this summary statement: *"The hypothesis is that the kind of order we know best, the order of purposive mind, is the ultimate explanation of the universe."*[15] Trueblood makes it quite clear that theism is distinct from pantheism on the one hand and subjectivism on the other. It is the conviction that God is both transcendent and immanent; the Creator of the world and yet One who is not confined to it. It is the view that God is not an "it," but One for whom we can honestly use not only the third person pronoun, but also the *second*. Whether one chooses to embrace theism or some secular world view the questions must still be asked: "Is the world more reasonably understood on this basis than on any other? Will this assumption best order all known facts into a reasonable whole?"[16]

The term theism is used as a convenient designation for a conception of Deity considered to be the single, personal, ultimate ground of the universe and source of all existence. Theism is opposed to a plurality of independent gods, to a metaphysical Absolute, to a limited, finite, emerging Deity, and to a deistic First Cause.[17] "Theism represents the Creator as the sovereign ruler of all things, and yet at work in the universe He has called into being. . . . He is distinct from the phenomenal order. As the intelligent self-conscious Will and the highest good, He is the living unity of existence and value, in vital relationship with his creation."[18]

In theism, however intimately God may be related to man, God is still God and man is still man. God is not the sum total of humanity, neither is he a mere idea in man's mind. Most theists affirm that God is the Conserver of absolute values, and that He is an adequate object of unqualified adoration or worship. God is not all that exists though he is the being from whom all others are derived. Some theists do not object to the use of "Absolute" as a term for God, the unconditioned being, "but only on the condition that the Absolute is not equated with all that really exists."[19]

Because we cannot escape the consciousness of our ultimate dependence, then the term God must also refer to "the Supreme Power in reality, that upon which we are all ultimately dependent."[20] The term does not suggest a physical thing or human person but it stands for something which is at least as real as any physical thing or human person.

The above concepts are theoretical, but so are all propositions which attempt to deal with the origin, meaning, or explanation of the universe and ultimate reality. Consideration will now be given to the rationale and evidences which appear to support the assumptions on which the theistic view is constructed.

Defense of the hypothesis. Certain philosophers such as Paul Tillich have argued about the futility of trying to prove God, or disprove him for that matter. And there are few who would claim that his existence or nonexistence is demonstrable. One must be cautious even about one's processes of reasoning to support the theistic world view. As John Baillie has observed, the attempt may be self-defeating since "it makes God seem less real than the means by which His existence is guaranteed."[21] Baillie continues:

> Let us consider what we do when we reach any reality by means of argument. Clearly what we do is to deduce this reality from some other reality which is already known to us. This other and previously known reality may in its turn have been deduced from a third reality our knowledge of which was again prior to our knowledge of the second.[22]

And in order to avoid infinite regress Baillie suggests: "There must be some reality by which we are directly confronted— some reality which we know, not because we know something else first, but rather is itself the ground of our knowledge of other things."[23] Somehow this reality is not necessarily known to us in isolation from all other realities, for in one sense nothing can be known by us out of relation to all other things. Professor Hocking once stated: "We as a group of human selves know that we are not alone in the universe; that is our first and persistent intuition."[24] This is at least a place to begin.

Before reason can ever function it must have data, raw materials, or statistics with which to work. Man's reason does not create an ongoing universe. There must be some kind of "givenness" as the starting point of all knowledge. Even then we cannot interpret our observations apart from some faith principle or assumption. A rational inference "requires at a minimum the faith that rational inference is trustworthy."[25] It is a matter of belief that objects exist independently of our senses and that causal relations between them occur, but this belief is necessary to organize our lives and thought.

Whether one is defending theism, humanism, or any other system, error will always occur whenever a half-truth gets passed off as if it were the whole truth. The mistake of every partial philosophy is that it seeks to make a single element in experience dominate or interpret the whole. Hopefully this pitfall will be avoided as the arguments in support of theism are examined.

One of the assumptions with which the theist begins is that the world is intelligible, and seemingly it becomes more intelligible the more we know about it. Following this there is another assumption—that we do not create this intelligibility but we discover it. The term natural law does not appear to furnish a complete or adequate explanation either of the sources or the purposive activity which we observe. The process of reasoning which we employ to relate, analyze, classify, and project either ideas or phenomena is referred to as a type of mental behavior. The theist believes that he can see in the universe evidence of such organizing factors. At this point he reasons from analogy. Calhoun presents a familiar illustration:

> If we come upon a situation which seems clearly to display intelligible or otherwise humanly appreciable or appropriable order which we have simply not read into it, and which cannot plausibly be accounted for as the outcome of known non-mental processes, it is a fair hypothesis that mental behavior in important respects like our own has helped to bring it about.[26]

This kind of reasoning is usually called the *teleological argument*, or the argument from design or purpose. One is aware of both strengths and weaknesses of the argument. Some argue that the "order" which we see in the universe is only apparent, and that such an arrangement could have occurred as a result of a random scattering of matter throughout space. One cannot conclusively refute this viewpoint but the theoretical probability of such an occurrence makes it most unreasonable. Though he looked on it with respect, Immanuel Kant had two criticisms of the argument from design. He believed that the argument could go no farther than to prove an architect or framer of the world, not a creator of matter. Second, he held that the existence of a strictly infinite being could not be demonstrated from a finite creation.

All that one can infer demonstratively is inconceivably vast power and wisdom. One must concede the validity of the second argument. The only answer is that the infinitude of God's attributes would follow if God is an unconditioned Being. At least glimpses of his attributes are disclosed in the order of the finite world. With respect to Kant's first criticism, if one will acknowledge that there is evidence for there being an Author of the amazing order which is seen in and through matter, there is at least the possibility that the framer of the world is also the author of matter itself. Whatever matter is, it cannot be separated from its properties, and such properties have yielded to the molding of this architect or framer of the world. Man can also use and shape this matter but he did not give to matter its initial properties. These could only have come from some ultimate, unconditioned cause.

It is quite true that the argument from design is an argument from analogy. Such an argument can neither be final nor conclusive but it appears to give some indication of a Mind behind the material universe. John Stuart Mill, however, maintained that the argument from design was a genuine instance of inductive reasoning. He wrote:

The design argument is not drawn from mere resemblance in nature to the work of human intelligence, but from the special character of this resemblance. The circumstances in which it is alleged that the world resembles the works of man are not circumstances taken at random, but are particular instances of a circumstance which experience shows to have real connection with an intelligent origin, the fact of conspiring to an end. The argument, therefore, is not one of mere analogy. As mere analogy it has weight, but it is more than analogy. It surpasses analogy exactly as induction surpasses it. It is an inductive argument.[27]

However, granting that the argument points to a Mind as the best explanation of the natural world it does not show that this Mind is now concerned about its creation, neither does it show that this Mind is a personal Being. But if there is an Author of the universe then this would represent a serious blow to any naturalistic philosophy.

Somewhat related to, but perhaps less refined than the argument from design is the *cosmological argument* which basically has to do with a First Cause. The argument was used by Plato and has been popular with theists for centuries. It, too, has its limitations but is worthy of consideration.

When most of us were rather small children we had an inquisitive nature. We wanted explanations for most everything we saw or heard in our world. The answers we received satisfied us for a while, but as we matured we learned that the world was extremely complex and that there were questions to which we could receive no satisfying answers. Often there was no concurrence in answers given by our wisest and most educated men. We continue to probe for causes and answers. Some years ago while I was taking an oral examination at an eastern university a professor addressed this question to me: "What do you do with the problem of God and infinite regress?" He was asking of course: "If God made the world, who made God?" My answer was: "I believe that God stands outside the cycle of infinite regress." He knew that I had as much right to that position as he did to the position that matter is eternal. His position was no escape from the problem of infinite regress.

Perhaps the above example will help us to focus on the substance of the cosmological argument. We keep searching for the cause of something which in turn was the cause of something else. Man's thirst for knowledge is insatiable. We continue our quest for reasons and explanations. But after a while, through weariness or indifference, we are content with the temporal solution and we forget to ask about ultimate origins. There are occasions, however, following an accident, tragedy, or bereavement, or following some unusual breakthrough in scientific achievement, when we return to our original questions as to why we are here, or why is the world here.

The cosmological argument is made to rest on the principle of causation. That is, whatever comes into being must owe its being to a cause not itself. The argument of course is not demonstrable, but neither is there any satisfaction in the hypothesis of an infinite series or regress. The causal argument insists that if there is a contingent being, it follows of necessity that there is a necessary being. Our own existence cannot be explained without reference to something or somebody outside of us as, for example, our parents. But a "necessary" being means a being that must exist and cannot not-exist. It is one thing to say that every object has a phenomenal cause and then insist that there is an infinity of the series of the causes. But merely saying that there is a series of phenomenal causes is not a sufficient explanation of the series. The series must somehow have a transcendent cause.

The substance of the cosmological argument is that God is a "sufficient" answer. This is an answer which requires no further answer for the existence of the universe. By the term God we mean One who is completely self-sufficient. He exists necessarily, a being who is self-caused and self-originating.

As to how a being can be the cause of itself, the necessary cause of all causes, and the final explanation of all explanations, we do not know. The argument is not compelling and such a being may not exist. But the alternatives open to us are somewhat limited. We might say that the world is without reason; it is inexplicable. Yet the presupposition of science is the rationality of nature. Every new advance in science follows some further discovery of the rational order that pervades the universe. One might argue that the world contains its own reason for being. But this view is hardly an improvement over the position we have presented and it is taken seriously by very few. Another alternative would be to view the world as under the control of a throng of divinities, each active and dominant within a province of its own. If a plurality of self-existing beings were possible then they would either have to be in concord or in conflict. If they were in concord then we would have to conclude that there are more causes for a given effect than are necessary. If they should be in conflict then they would not be dominant in any particular province. Philosophically, a plurality of all-powerful deities is impossible. Furthermore, scientific observation tends to show that the world is a cosmos and if there is one coherent system pervading the universe then it is more reasonable to assume that the operations of the universe spring from one sufficient cause.

If the world is not self-explanatory then "the only truly

sufficient explanation for the existence of *anything* is the existence of *something* which is necessary. And the only kind of Being we are ever tempted to call necessary is God."[28] According to our argument, there is no known sufficient reason for the world apart from God.

Though the above reasoning is not always convincing it does merit serious consideration. We shall find a strong similarity between this approach and what is known as the *ontological argument* which follows.

The ontological argument. The basic structure of the ontological argument was produced by Anselm of Canterbury in the eleventh century. The validity of the argument was challenged not only by Anselm's contemporaries, but it has come under attack by theologians and philosophers ever since. Some philosophers, however, give considerable credence to the argument. Professor Whitehead apparently believed that the only possible proof for the existence of God seemed to rest on ontological proof, but he recognized that most philosophers were reluctant to accept this. Many have obviously shared the view of Bertrand Russell who once said that it is easier to feel that the argument must be erroneous than to say exactly wherein the error lies.

The ontological argument affirms that the existence of God is involved in the very idea of God. And the "proofs" begin and end with the analysis of the idea. Anselm argued that the greatest or the most perfect *conceivable* being must be actual or have objective being. If it did not have, then any actual being or property would be greater than what was *conceived* to be the most perfect. For Anselm, God is "the Being, than which no greater can be conceived." In answer to this contention it is argued that existence is not necessarily a constituent of a concept. Or, if one puts it another way, the existence of a *thing* cannot be concluded from the definition of a word. But according to Anselm, one must think about the Being than which no greater can be conceived as actually existing, for if one should conceive of him as not existing, then he has not been thinking of the greatest conceivable Being.

Professor Charles Hartshorne, who is more of a Panentheist, has considerable respect for the ontological argument.

In a dialogue published in *Religious Experience and Truth*, Professor Hartshorne was asked the question: "Does the term *God* have a referent?" and Hartshorne answered:

> The reply is that if it does not, then there is a logical flaw in the conception. For this name, unlike all others, by its barest connotation, requires a denotation, so that he who denies the latter implies a logical defect in the former. If, however, there be such defect, then God cannot exist; if there be none, then he cannot fail to exist.[29]

The question of divinity, according to Hartshorne, is so fundamental that even the basic rules of our language must either require or exclude God. He states: "Either all conceivable facts properly understood must manifest God's existence, or no conceivable facts or state of affairs could manifest it. This is the choice—all else is talk, not about God, but about some idol or fetish."[30]

It was the view of Paul Tillich that the ontological argument points to the ontological structure of finitude by showing that man's awareness of finitude includes an awareness of the infinite. The question of God is implied in the finite structure of being. This is much the same as the view of Descartes who held that the idea of an infinite self-conscious being is deduced from our own finite self-consciousness. Such an idea could not be a product of the finite self. The presence of the idea in the human mind could be accounted for only by ascribing it to the Infinite Being himself.[31]

Whatever credibility the above arguments may have, they still do not bring us to a Christian conception of God. The ontological argument points up the fact that man's very awareness of finitude shows that in some sense he has an awareness of the infinite. If a concept of the infinite is a concept of perfection, then the ontological argument gives plausibility to the existence of the most perfect Being. And yet the argument leaves us with an abstraction which may or may not be the personal God of theism.

The cosmological argument is significant in that it suggests a world Artisan whose existence accounts for the being and orderly change of the world. The teleological argument focuses attention on the intelligence of this World Planner who is responsible for the harmonies which pervade the order of nature. But even these arguments fail to reveal to us a God of justice and mercy. They are reasonable but they are not compelling.

There are some who look upon the *moral argument* for God as being a more adequate explanation of the kind of power which must be at the heart of the universe. Early formulations of the argument were set forth by Immanuel Kant. Though he had previously challenged the traditional arguments for God's existence, Kant now structured a new approach to theism based upon moral experience. His whole moral system was an emphasis upon duty. He conceived of moral experience as an absolute and universal experience of obligation to respect persons. Human beings must be treated as ends rather than means.

Though men are not equal in physical gifts or mental endowments, one must recognize the essential equality of all persons in moral matters. Kant's *Categorical Imperative* was an unconditional command. It was not to be qualified by some "if" or "might" or other contingency. This imperative was the voice of duty, the imperative of morality, namely, "Act only on that principle which thou canst will should become a universal law." It says simply, "Do right." We see that Kant's moral law was very close to the Golden Rule of Jesus. It is a law that has emerged in almost every culture where men have given consideration to the bases of moral action.

Nothing should be called good, without qualifications, according to Kant, except a good will. A good will may be defined as a will to do what ought to be done. To say that something "is" does not mean the same thing as saying that something "ought" to be. The word ought is crucial for it implies freedom of the will. In a completely determined world there could be no sense of "ought." As Kant developed his case for the moral law he believed that *three* postulates were necessary to make moral experience possible. They are (1) freedom, (2) immortality, and (3) God. Kant assumed that the moral law demanded an ultimate proportioning of happiness to worth. No such balance is seen in this world. Man has visions of righteousness which are beyond his achievement here and now. Kant held that it is more reasonable to believe that there is another world beyond this in which the consequences of moral judgment will be brought to light.

If one follows the reasoning of Kant then he can move on to his final point, that God is a postulate of the moral law. Because man belongs to the world and is dependent on it, he will never produce by his own power a happiness that is truly proportionate to morality. "Therefore," says Kant, "the *summum bonum*, the union of virtue and happiness, is possible in the world only on the supposition of a Supreme Being having a causality corresponding to moral character." Kant went further and said that the three postulates of freedom, immortality, and the existence of God all proceed from the principle of morality which is itself not a postulate but a law, an imperative. The presence of moral law, to Kant, simply implied a Lawgiver. God is necessary to harmonize what is and what ought to be. And he will ultimately proportion happiness to worthiness.

The moral law is viewed as absolutely sacred.

Kant loves to dwell on its awful sublimity. . . . Absolute truthfulness, absolute respect for the rights and freedom of every one of your fellow men, with devotion to the cause of high-mindedness, of honesty, of justice, of simplicity, of honor—such is Kant's ideal, and so far as in him lay, he was always true to it.[32]

Men were struggling with the concept of value long before Kant. The Greeks usually spoke of three forms of value: the good, the true, and the beautiful. If a conflict arose, moral considerations took precedence over the aesthetic. To Plato, moral value resides not in acts or actions, but in a certain type of character—the righteous character. We still look back to Socrates, Plato's master, as one who preferred to lose his life rather than his integrity. He knew that if he should lose at this point he would lose his "soul," something more precious than material possession or physical existence.

The vast proportion of our living is in the world of things, held together in mechanical and mathematical relations. But most of us do not interpret all of our experiences in terms of physics and chemistry. We know that there are levels of life which transcend an animal's appetitive nature. The scientist who commits himself in the struggle for truth, defends his freedom to find the truth, and is moved to share the truth with others, is pursuing moral insights.

It may be true that "fact" experience is one thing and value experience another, but this tends to pose a false contrast between fact and value, as though a fact were real and value no more than a subjective opinion. No amount of factual knowledge describing what *is* will ever be sufficient in itself to determine what *ought* to be the case in any given situation. Scientific investigation may predict what course of action is needed to arrive at some particular objective, but it is beyond the domain of science to state what objectives and desires men *should* have.

Is man living in two distinct worlds; the world of what *is* and *must* be and the world of *ought* and *should* be? Is there no underlying unity or purpose between the two, or are they different aspects of one world? Some would hold, as Plato suggested, that the Good gives unity to all there is. Others who are sensitive to beauty and goodness refuse to believe that there is sufficient evidence for any type of moral unity in the world. They are convinced that men ought to be good but they contend that "goodness" is a relative term and it involves nothing more than mere subjective reference.

Here we find one of the major objections to the moral argument. Men differ widely on ethical questions. It is assumed, therefore, that "good" and "bad," "right" and "wrong" are only subjective terms expressing individual taste. Our problem will be to examine whether ethical propositions are genuine propositions, i.e., are they capable of being true or false?

In spite of conflicting views on moral issues we still find a great measure of consensus. "The best evidence for ethical objectivity . . . [is] the fact that there is really a significant agreement in moral convictions, an agreement too great to be accounted for by coincidence. The convergence of ethical testimony is parallel to the convergence of opinion regarding physical factors."[33]

The same argument is pressed by Professor Bertocci. The proponent for the moral argument goes beyond an appeal to intuition. "Asking for no concessions, he insists that his case is based on the same kind of logic which leads philosophers to grant the reality of the physical world."[34] The point here is that although we cannot always trust every sense perception, we don't deny the validity of sense perception generally. "We reason," as Bertocci says, "that those perceptions most consistent with other perceptions are to be taken as true. In other words, coherence among sense-perceptions is our test of truth. In this way we build our 'physical world.' "[35] Why should this type of reasoning be acceptable in scientific endeavor but not allowed in testing moral judgments?

The argument is pressed further by Bertocci. He notes the assumptions involved in acquiring scientific evidence. There is (1) the assumption of the general validity of sense-experience, (2) the assumption of the validity of our logical and inductive reasoning, and (3) the very basic assumption that truth is worthwhile. Now truth is a value, and though we never have all the truth, we are persuaded that without truth there can be no adequate adjustment to the world. If one argues that all value judgments are simply projections of our feelings or wishes, then, since truth is a value, it too is a projection and nothing more. To continue in this direction brings one to complete skepticism. If one is to be consistent he should not trust his thinking about nature unless he also trusts his thinking about values. The point is that if the "belief in the validity of values is a delusion, the belief in the validity of science is also a delusion, since it rests on the conviction that truth is valuable."[36]

Because there is often disagreement about intuitions of value, this does not mean that our moral faculties are never to be trusted. We do not lose faith in our sensory processes just because we occasionally "see" something that is not there. Though our moral judgments are not always easy to check, we should not for that reason discard the general validity of the moral consciousness. We know that "with the growth of sensitiveness and the development of the human mind, the difference of judgment concerning both the moral and the material order is greatly diminished."[37]

We return again to the conclusion of Kant stated earlier. If we assume that values are not irrelevant to the world order, then we may find in the universe something which supports the interrelation of values and natural processes. Yet how is such an interrelation possible? It is conceivable if one postulates a Supreme Purposer who is the ultimate source of values, persons, and nature. Values such as truth, goodness, and beauty only have meaning when they are associated with persons. Whatever is beautiful is beautiful for somebody; anything true is true for somebody, anything good, in the basic sense, is good for somebody. If values are relevant to the world order they must find their relevance in Somebody.

The moral argument leads us to an interpretation of the world which gives meaning to both values and existence. As Bertocci reasons, "Human beings at their best plan their activities in accordance with values. Why not follow this analogy and postulate a cosmic Being whose very nature is to be intelligent and good, whose eternal purposes gradually take concrete shape in the course of cosmic and human history."[38] According to this argument the world-order is directed by a conscious rational Being who wills the final triumph of goodness. This view is the counter conception of humanism which can only see a universe that is wholly indifferent to truth, goodness, and love.

GOD AS PERSONAL
Whenever we begin to explore the world of values we find reason to believe that we are moving very close to the heart of things and approaching ultimate meanings. To find goodness instead of a blind process behind the universe is to come very close to God.

If our reasoning about values is valid then the conclusion is that the Ground of the world is moral. From this point it is not difficult to conceive that it is also personal. Goodness, truth, and love exist only in personal life. There is no goodness except in some personal will that holds to what is true and just. Love has no meaning in the abstract. It is given meaning by personal beings who love.

To speak of God as personal is a stumbling block to many humanists, nontheists, and some Christians as well. Our difficulty is that we cannot describe God by comparing him with anything else of the same kind. All of our human thought of God is inevitably in symbols. These symbols are found in the world of our experience. Our worthiest symbols are those that express personality at its highest. No word or idea which we can apply to God can be really appropriate. What symbol or term taken from our own human experience would be adequate to describe or express the Infinite? Surely the category of personality is the least inadequate.

In our experience the term personal is associated with finiteness, limitation, and caprice, and such human weaknesses, it is argued, should not be attributed to God. Clearly, human limitations which are inherent in our physical existence do not apply to God. When we say that God is personal we are saying that God is more like a person than like a thing, more like a person than like a mathematical equation, more like a person than like a machine. And "personal" is a better word than "suprapersonal," because suprapersonal might lead us to think of him as impersonal. If we speak of the Infinite in abstract or impersonal terms, we unconsciously liken him to forces that are less vital and lower than ourselves. There are minimal personal characteristics which must apply to God. These are "awareness, intelligence, purposiveness, the capacity to appreciate, the capacity to respond to persons." As John Bennett says, "It is difficult to see how a God who lacks those qualities could be a fitting object of devotion or an adequate explanation of existence, or one to whom our conduct could make any difference."[39]

It is not conceivable that the impersonal reactions which we find in the physical world offer the clue to the nature of ultimate reality. "Mechanical uniformities," as Lynn Hough notes, "may be the servants of intelligence. They cannot be the creators of intelligence."[40] On the impersonal level, the presence of truth and error can never be understood. There is no way to account for the distinction between right and

tive Good Will trying to penetrate the barriers of flesh. Professor Rall has said:

> If there be a God like that of the Christian faith, personal, good, a living God and not an abstract idea or order or essence, then we should expect to know him best not in abstract principles or impersonal ideals, but in a living deed of history and in personal life. . . . This expression in a person has a vividness, an appeal, a power such as abstractions can never possess.[47]

We learn that God, in the New Testament, is more than a voice speaking from above or an arm reaching down in power. He is Love and Life and Spirit entering into man and dwelling in man. God was in Christ—not just in doctrines or miracles, or subjective experiences or religious forms. He was "in a historic person, in Christ's spirit, his word, his life, his death. . . . The historical, the human, the personal and ethical furnish the sphere in which the transcendent God becomes known; and God is here as deed not primarily as idea."[48]

It is the Christian faith that the living God has touched our life. "The greatest single fact of history is the breaking in of the life of God through this unique Life. Here at last the Love of God found complete expression."[49] Jesus is the challenge to men to trust in God as Father, as a creative living Spirit, as One whose power is accessible, dependable, and real. He is One who still works through the unfolding events of history. He is the God of all peoples. Man's faith is the acceptance of that challenge.

The acceptance of God's revelation is a matter of faith, just as the acceptance of an impersonal universe also is a matter of faith. If faith rests on no evidence, either empirical or rational, "then it may move off in any direction and there is no check upon it and no limitations to its claims. Faith, it appears, does go beyond evidence, but it moves in the direction in which the evidence or reason points."[50] For the Christian, there is abundant evidence that the Divine entered into human life directly. This was the great adventure of revelation showing how far love would go to secure the willing response of men.

One should try to avoid two extremes in interpreting the revelation of God. One extreme is to assume that propositional formulations of doctrine by themselves constitute the substance of God's disclosure. The other extreme is to rely solely on one's subjective experience and feelings as the essential elements in the understanding of God's purposes.

Christianity is many things. It is a way of life. It is a distinctive quality of individual and corporate experience. It involves the mind, the feelings, and the will. But it is also based on a body of belief. The Christian way of life cannot be permanently maintained without Christian belief. How can there be a demand for Christian living without an acceptance of the truth in Christian revelation? And yet how can one greatly believe and not at the same time deeply feel?

Our knowledge of God comes through his Son and through his word. And yet also, like all other knowledge, it must come by way of life. This is the knowledge of acquaintance, not the knowledge of information; it is knowing God and not merely knowing about God. For all practical purposes there is no revelation until the truth speaks to me. The historic fact of Jesus with all its meaning is just the beginning. Men come to know God through Christ, but this knowledge is enlarged as men are led into that life of fellowship with God which Jesus lived. They know more of God as they share that Spirit of God which was in Jesus.

It is clear that certain beliefs about God's revelation must be upheld as true if we are to mean anything definite by Christianity at all. But faith is more than the holding of correct doctrines. Some personal fellowship must be established with the God who has revealed himself. The essence of revelation, as William Temple has said, is "intercourse of mind and event, not the communication of doctrine distilled from that intercourse."[51] In part, what we are trying to say is that along with the truth of revelation, there ought to be the experience of revelation. Martin Buber has written:

One can lead no one to real faith, but one can show another the face of real faith, show it so clearly that he will not henceforth confuse faith with its artful ape, "religious" feeling. And one can teach him *with what* one believes when one really believes: with the lived moment and ever again with the lived moment.[52]

In one sense revelation is not self-validating, but if it is asked to authenticate itself, it can do nothing but offer its own credentials. Authentication through miracle and fulfilled prophecy can still be justified, but there is another approach which compels our respect. It is noted by Temple:

> The evidence of God's special activity is indeed not to be found in what baffles the intelligence, but rather in power active for such purposes as may reasonably be supposed divine. Where power and mercy are combined, there is God manifest; where we see righteousness or love, we see the character of God; where we see these triumphing, there we see God in action; where we see them achieve their purpose despite all calculable probabilities, there we acknowledge God signally self-revealed.[53]

There is a sense in which all is of God, as Temple says, "but not all things equally display His character. . . . If God makes Himself known, we shall expect to find progress in man's apprehension of Him. . . . If He is active in the progress, the progress must bear the marks of His continuing guidance."[54] These, according to Temple, are the marks of a true revelation.

The testimony of history is significant, but it is equally important to know what God is doing now. In the Gospels Jesus tells us that God still lives, that he works until now, he still forgives, he still offers his grace and love, he still supports man in the decisions of life, and he still brings man into fellowship with himself. These convictions remain a part of the Christian faith. The Divine was revealed in word and in Life, and it is our persuasion that in him, men still live, move, and have their being.

6

IN CONCLUSION

"I hold that at the heart of genuine Christianity are certain truths which have already once saved Western civilization, and judiciously employed, may save it again."   —Irving Babbitt[1]

Some years ago George A. Gordon observed that "the meaning of the times does not lie in the times themselves, but in the ideal forces behind them and that work through them."[2] We have suggested in this study that the real "religion" of modern man is secular humanism. We have tried to examine this philosophy and evaluate the basic theories which have gained for it such popular and enthusiastic devotion. No doubt we have fallen short of the pattern once suggested by Professor Whitehead of "balancing the fact, the theory, the alternatives, and the ideal," but we trust that there has been some clarification of the essential features as well as the limitations of this modern faith.

   With man's enormously increased knowledge of his world and an almost incredible mastery over nature, the secular humanist believes that God becomes unnecessary and practically worthless as an explanatory principle behind the world. Secular humanists usually offer four major considerations in support of their atheism, as noted by Professor Schilling. These are: "(1) the opposition between scientific method and religious belief; (2) the extent of human suffering; (3) the negative effect of religious belief on the struggle for human justice; and (4) the tendency of theistic belief to diminish human responsibility."[3] Most outspoken antitheistic humanists make plain their conviction that the priority which they give to the dignity of man can be guaranteed only by the absence of God.[4]

In spite of the widespread acceptance of humanistic theories, we have tried to note specific areas in which this system fails to measure up as a philosophy by which men should regulate their lives. Final causes seem never to be considered. "Why is there a universe? What is its purpose? For the humanist these questions are meaningless, because their answers require something above and beyond man's own experience."[5] Because naturalism is an impersonal view of the universe it cannot of itself explain the personal. When humanists hold to a strictly naturalistic view of the nature of man, and then acknowledge that man has the ability to reason, to love, and to create, they are endowing man with attributes which they claim are absent in the rest of the universe.

Humanists who rely so heavily on the disciplines of modern science often forget that there is no way of securing objective truth except "by the way of subjective conviction."[6] Or, to put it in the words of Francis McConnell, "The greater concerns of life move along on a basis of belief."[7] The humanist appears to be inconsistent in not following through on the presuppositions of science which include the orderliness and intelligibility of the universe. It seems strange that many humanists will accept these premises and then conclude that ultimately the universe is irrational and that there is no meaning behind nature's laws.

When one assumes that by denying God he has absolved himself from all metaphysical puzzles, he usually finds that he has not solved his difficulties but has added to them. Humanists can never reach God as a conclusion when all the premises of their arguments exclude him. To exclude God from life and then try to find him by logical process will always be a vain quest. Discussing the limitations of both the religious and scientific approaches, Julian Huxley, though highly partial to the role of science, has some words of caution to those who rest their case on the disciplines of science: "Perhaps . . . Science has sometimes made the further error of mistaking firm knowledge for complete knowledge, and neglecting to see the real facts in which religion has her being."[8] While suggesting that in the future religion must abandon the intellectual arrogance of its theology, Huxley says that the chief task of organized science

> will be to enlarge its bounds, admit that the highest flights of the human spirit are as much realities as the routine activities of the human body, or the doings of the atoms and molecules of lifeless matter, to recognize for what they are the realities on which the religious life is based, to see religion's values.[9]

Man must resist the temptation, says Rufus Jones, to narrow "knowledge." Rather, "We must include under the *knowledge-process* our entire capacity for dealing with reality."[10] There is a sense in which the significance of man lies within the circle of his own activities and experience, but finally he is forced beyond himself for the full account of himself.

Many humanists are trying to find an ethic which will conserve the genuinely human values. But ethical and moral relativism provides no reasonable value structure. In the world view which they have embraced human values have no enduring quality. Whatever values the humanists try to preserve have to be fastened on the outside of a philosophy which really contradicts them.

It is unfortunate that much humanism today disavows the theistic world view for which early humanists had such respect. Many of the social ideals and principles of justice found in modern humanism were seen much earlier in biblical religion. Humanists have inherited many of their ideas and sentiments concerning human dignity and the well-being of man from a faith which they now largely discredit. John Reid says:

> The problem may not be that God is uninteresting or without importance but that those through whom He speaks, or rather who claim to speak for Him, are unattractive and unconvincing as human beings. . . . The complacency of the unbeliever, his indifference to religious values, is an appropriate, or at least an understandable, reaction to the uninspiring and even disedifying example of those who claim supreme importance for these values. The pretensions of Christians are lofty, but their lives are not conspicuously

free of ambition and ruthlessness, selfishness, smugness, self-justification, and dishonesty. The unbeliever need not insist that the faithful are worse than others; it is enough that he finds them no better.[11]

As Reid points out, "One is quick to see the absurdity of a faith which is so invisible that it makes no difference, and is simply conformed in every respect to the ordinary world."[12]

Humanists tell us that the theistic tree must be judged by its social fruits, and often these are found to be unpalatable. In *The Catholic World*, November 1968, Gary Schouberg writes:

> Unfortunately, many Christians have abused the hearing given them and wasted the time of people who trusted them enough to listen to what they had to say. For that reason, it is quite understandable that many people today listen to Christians with only the slightest patience and greatest skepticism. The Christian's life must be humanly believable so that he will be given the hearing necessary to communicate what he really believes. Only until such communication is achieved can Christ through human history confront the non-Christian in his most radical self-hood and invite him to follow him.[13]

The Christian cannot ignore these indictments, and he will do well to heed the further admonition:

> Let those who believe in Christ understand that proclaiming Him as living in them involves a presence that is ineradicable. . . . A Christian communicates his faith primarily through the way he lives and only secondarily through what he professes to believe. . . . The world is well advised to pray only if those who do pray communicate a joy and a strength which nothing else can give.[14]

Yet, it is always possible that many who are obsessed with secular humanist ideology have been sucked into what John Courtney Murray calls "the atheism of distraction—people who are just 'too damn busy' to worry about God at all." But whatever the reason, millions of people are completely indifferent to theistic faith. Many of these same people, however, often find nothing in humanistic theories that will help them to face their frustrations, hardships, and unhappiness. They have been told by some humanists that these evils would gradually disappear from society as the level of education increased. Yet history has borne out the fact that often, under more highly developed systems of education, man has sometimes become more ingeniously diabolic.

There were humanists fifty years ago who were looking forward to the time when, in its full maturity, science would "merit the mastery of the world." We find ourselves today almost in the grip of such a mastery, and no one laments its inadequacy more strongly than the scientist. After World War I, H. G. Wells believed that his task was to teach mankind the basic tenets of humanism—"the history of man's progress, the story of scientific advance, and the achievements and possibilities of social salvation." But, as Kingsley Martin has said, "in the end he despaired. Fascism and World War II were the final blow. In his old age, when the bombs were falling he wrote that mind had 'reached the end of its tether.' "[15] The secular humanist does his share of whistling in the dark, as John Reid says, whenever he minimizes the darker facets of human existence, those about which man seems powerless to accomplish anything in the way of correction or deliverance.[16]

The humanist's road to the future is a perilously uncertain one, writes Gareth Jones. Man is all alone and a precipice is near. The gap between the optimistic side of humanism and the down-to-earth application of principles is a fundamental weakness in humanism—a weakness that plagues mankind.[17]

The human mind hates meaninglessness, and yet the secular humanist tells man that the highest good he can know in this life has no lasting significance. There is nothing in the universe which can acknowledge or preserve man's noblest aspirations. Leslie Weatherhead uses the illustration of a large ship in the middle of the ocean on a long sea voyage. If the captain were to announce that there was plenty of food to eat, plenty of drink, and that life would go on as usual, however he had decided not to make for port, but he would just cruise around and around until the fuel was exhausted and then he would sink the ship—such a speech would have snatched from every mind the concept of purpose, meaning, and goal.[18] Life can have no significance if everything is to disappear in a meaningless flux at the last.

When the humanist says that there is no objective status to values beyond man there appears to be an inherent contradiction in his position. He affirms truth as a value, yet there seems to be nothing in nature to give rise to such a value. The question as to how nature undirected by any cosmic purpose could impose upon man such a value concept is left unanswered. This question may appear irrelevant to the humanist, but to the theist this looks like an evasion of a very basic issue.[19] There is no valid reason for anyone being careful about the truth in the fundamentally impersonal world of humanism. But in a personal world there is great reason to be careful about the truth, says Trueblood, "since dishonesty means taking advantage of the trust of others."[20] Furthermore it would be disloyalty to the One who is the source of man's personal being.

If we would persuade the next generation to believe in God, then we must strive to form and interpret experience so that such belief will arise. God is not just another name for the totality of things. Neither can he be regarded as the impersonal soul of an impersonal universe. He is not an entity which we may add to or subtract from according to scientific formulations and procedures. God is himself the condition of scientific knowledge, as Arthur Balfour has stated. This point is pressed further:

> If He be excluded from the causal series which produces belief, the cognitive series which justifies them is corrupted at the root. And as it is only in a theistic setting that beauty can retain its deepest meaning, and love its brightest lustre, so these great truths of aesthetics and ethics are but half-truths, isolated and imperfect, unless we add to them yet a third. We must hold that reason and the works of reason have their source in God; that from Him they draw their inspiration; and that if they repudiate their origin, by this very act they proclaim their own insufficiency.[21]

As a theist the Christian is often tempted to embrace popular moods and accept pseudo solutions to human problems, but he eventually comes back to questions of purpose, values, and ultimate meaning. He is persuaded that "man does not live by social reconstruction alone."[22] The Christian is convinced that even with all the difficulties of theistic faith (see note 23 on page 121), it is still the most coherent interpretation of experience available. It achieves a more adequate synthesis of "all the facts" than other world views.

In theism men find a philosophy of the universe which they believe more adequately accounts for both the natural order and for man's highest moral and spiritual aspirations. George Gordon once wrote, "Nature has something to say for God, not a great deal to be sure, but nevertheless an authentic and significant utterance. She is not her own; she belongs to another; of her Owner she is a manifestation, and her final meaning is found in the terms of his life."[24]

We know that the universe is immeasurably larger than anything the imagination can conceive, but the theist affirms this "message" of nature—that the world owes its existence to the volitional act of God. Yet the Christian is persuaded that in other ways God has disclosed himself. The earth has beheld a unique figure in whose life many can see the supreme moral achievement of flesh and blood. In this historic Person, in his life, his words, his cross, his resurrection—the Christian is confident that he has the surest clue to the nature and the character of God.

The Christian can see man's weakness, suffering, sorrow, and exploitation, but he remembers that the Creator has spoken to these conditions, and he has also acted. He has chosen to share man's burden and to take his place alongside this frail, tragic, yet glorious creation. With this faith the Christian gradually loses his apprehension about the future. He is assured that the values he has trusted are secure in the mind and life of God, because in God these values live.

Without this perspective of the future, the humanist can only view such a faith as a religion of losers. Man may be optimistic about social betterment, but apart from this, and from any objective standpoint, whatever men have managed to put together they are going to lose. They are being wiped out, losing all that they could ever hope to have. On the other hand, despite the meaninglessness of it all, the Christian is sure that another word has come to man. How do you win? You win by losing. There is a redemption of the values which men have held. There is something in the universe that sustains and protects these values in an appropriate way.

The Bible offers guidance for the most practical issues of our day. It outlines safeguards of human life, family life, personal property, and personal integrity. For human life—"You must not murder." For family life—"You must not commit adultery." For personal property—"You must not steal." For personal integrity—"You must not lie." These principles were engraven not only on tablets of stone, but they lie embedded in human experience and in human history.[25] It is doubtful if secular men are offering secular man reasonable substitutes, or a wisdom superior to these precepts.

The Christian must assume the integrity of the nontheistic humanist who looks on a world without God. But the humanist should also respect the theist who is willing to allow into his frame of reference testimony which is neither absurd nor irrational. To the Christian, God is not a theorem.

God is the guarantor against meaninglessness in existence, the supreme object of human devotion, the unifier of human values, the inspirer of moral obligation, the breaker of self-will, the restorer of man to new life, the raiser of the common life from routine to service, the source of hope for fulfilled existence.[26]

A number of years ago Arthur Balfour wrestled with the same subject we have been discussing. His evaluation of humanistic faith is clear.

Does it offer consolation to those who are in grief, hope to those who are bereaved, strength to the weak, forgiveness to the sinful, rest to those who are weary and heavy laden? If not, then whatever be its merits, it is no rival to Christianity. It cannot penetrate and vivify the inmost life of ordinary humanity. There is in it no nourishment for ordinary human souls, no comfort for ordinary human sorrow, no help for ordinary human weakness. Not less than the crudest irreligion does it leave us men divorced from all communion

with God, face to face with the unthinking energies of
nature which gave us birth, and into which, if supernatural
religion indeed be a dream, we must after a few fruitless
struggles be again dissolved.[27]

Man's world must be viewed either as merely human, or
else as a cooperative undertaking of the human and the divine.
These alternatives are not finespun cobwebs of speculation,
says Edgar Brightman. "They reach into the deepest needs
of the human soul, into the sources of life's hopes, and life's
meaning; and the choice of one alternative or the other will
probably do more to affect the total perspective of a person's
outlook on life than any other choice he can make."[28]

The French, Nobel-prizewinning author, François Mauriac,
who died in 1970, provided his own eulogy in a recording he
made twenty years prior to his death. "I believe," he said, "as
I did as a child, that life has meaning, a direction, a value;
that no suffering is lost, that every tear counts, each drop of
blood, that the secret of the world is to be found in St. John's
'Deus caritas est'—'God is love.' "[29] If God is Love, then the
story of the cross brings this home to us in a better way than
all of our conceptual language can.

NOTES

Preface
1. Karl Jaspers, *Man in the Modern Age* (New York: Double-day, 1957), pp. 15-16.
2. Martin E. Marty, "The Problem of God," *Ladies' Home Journal,* Dec. 1969, p. 128.
3. Georgia Harkness, *Stability Amid Change* (Nashville: Abingdon Press, 1969), p. 111.
4. Lynn H. Hough, *The Christian Criticism of Life* (Nashville: Abingdon-Cokesbury Press, 1941), pp. 181-82. Used by permission.

1   Humanism: The Real Religion of Modern Man
1. From *The Protestant Era* by Paul Tillich (Chicago: University of Chicago Press, 1948), p. 267. Used by permission of Robert C. Kimball.
2. Quoted in Michael Novak, *Belief and Unbelief* (New York: New American Library, 1965), p. 151. Used by permission.
3. Martin Marty, *Varieties of Unbelief* (New York: Doubleday, 1964), p. 42.
4. Oscar Blackwelder, in his exposition of Galatians, *The Interpreter's Bible* (Nashville: Abingdon Press, 1953), 10:497.
5. D. Elton Trueblood, *Philosophy of Religion* (New York: Harper & Row, 1957), p. xi. Used by permission.
6. H. J. Blackham, ed., *Objections to Humanism (*Philadelphia: Lippincott, 1965), p. 27.

7. Ibid., p. 108.
8. Michael Novak, "The Society of Lonely People," *Ladies' Home Journal,* Dec. 1969, p. 129.
9. Jacques Maritain, *Integral Humanism* (New York: Charles Scribner's Sons, 1968), p. 90. Used by permission.
10. Novak, *Belief and Unbelief,* p. 153.

2   Varieties of Humanism

1. Crane Brinton, *Ideas and Men* (Englewood Cliffs, N.J.: Prentice-Hall, 1950), p. 263.
2. Ibid., p. 262.
3. Lynn H. Hough, *The Christian Criticism of Life* (Nashville: Abingdon-Cokesbury Press, 1941), p. 284. Used by permission.
4. Jacques Maritain, *Integral Humanism* (New York: Charles Scribner's Sons, 1968), p. 23. Used by permission.
5. Hough, *The Christian Criticism of Life,* pp. 284ff.
6. Preparatory Notes to *La Sainte Famille,* Karl Marx: *Morceaux Choisis* (Paris: Gallimard, 1934), p. 229; as quoted by Maritain, *Integral Humanism,* p. 47.
7. Maritain, *Integral Humanism,* p. 61.
8. *Pravda,* May 17, 1934.
9. Maritain, *Integral Humanism,* p. 84.
10. Ibid., p. 36.
11. Ibid., p. 60.
12. Ibid., p. 88.
13. Albert William Levi, *Humanism and Politics* (Bloomington, Ind.: Indiana University Press, 1969), pp. 453ff.
14. John Dewey, *A Common Faith* (New Haven, Conn.: Yale University Press, 1934), p. 1.
15. Arthur Hazard Dakin, *Man the Measure* (Princeton: Princeton University Press, 1939), p. 255.
16. Erich Fromm, *Man for Himself* (New York: Holt, Rinehart & Winston, 1947), p. 53. Used by permission.
17. Ibid., p. 162.
18. "A Humanist Manifesto," *The New Humanist,* May-June 1933. Used by permission.
19. Corliss Lamont, *The Philosophy of Humanism* (New York: Frederick Ungar Publishing Co., 1949), p. 14.

3   The Strength of Humanism

1. Irving Babbitt, *On Being Creative* (Boston: Houghton Mifflin Co., 1932), p. xvii.
2. Frederic Seebohm, *The Oxford Reformers* (New York: E. P. Dutton & Co., 1914), pp. 208ff. Cf. Hugh Watts, "Humanists," *Encyclopedia of Religion and Ethics* (New York: Charles Scribner's Sons, 1955), 6:831-36.
3. Julian S. Huxley, *Religion Without Revelation* (New York: New American Library, 1959), pp. 370, 372. Used by permission.
4. Hamilton Fyfe, "Humanism As a World Unifying Force," *The Humanist,* 1953, p. 13.
5. Georgia Harkness, *The Modern Rival of Christian Faith* (Nashville: Abingdon Press, 1952), p. 81.
6. John Reid, *Man Without God* (Philadelphia: Westminster Press, 1971), p. 90.
7. Ibid., p. 78.
8. Attributed to Robert G. Ingersoll.
9. Huxley, *Religion Without Revelation,* p. 357.
10. Ibid., pp. 380-81.
11. Erich Fromm, *Psychoanalysis and Religion* (New Haven, Conn.: Yale University Press, 1950), p. 9; cf. pp. 139ff.
12. S. Paul Schilling, *God in an Age of Atheism* (Nashville: Abingdon Press, 1969), pp. 89-90. Used by permission.

4   The Inadequacy of Humanism

1. Bertrand Russell, "A Free Man's Worship," from *The Basic Writings of Bertrand Russell,* ed. Robert E. Egner and Lester E. Denonn (New York: Simon & Schuster, 1961), p. 67. Copyright © 1961 by George Allen & Unwin, Ltd. Used by permission.
2. Max C. Otto, *Things and Ideals* (New York: Henry Holt & Co., 1924), p. 289. Used by permission of Holt, Rinehart and Winston, Inc.
3. Corliss Lamont in *Objections to Humanism,* ed. H. J. Blackham (Philadelphia: Lippincott, 1965), p. 23.
4. Nowell Smith in *Objections to Humanism,* p. 24.
5. Martin Marty, *Varieties of Unbelief* (New York: Doubleday, 1964), p. 44.

6. Blackham, *Objections to Humanism,* pp. 122-23.
7. Ronald Hepburn, "A Critique of Humanist Theology," *Objections to Humanism,* p. 48.
8. Corliss Lamont, *The Philosophy of Humanism* (New York: Frederick Ungar Publishing Co., 1949), p. 13.
9. Bertrand Russell, "What I Believe," *The Nation,* Apr. 29, 1931, 133:43.
10. Paul Arthur Schilpp, ed., *The Philosophy of Bertrand Russell* (Evanston and Chicago: Northwestern University Press, 1944), p. 722. Used by permission.
11. Bertrand Russell, "Reply to Criticisms," *The Philosophy of Bertrand Russell,* p. 720.
12. Ibid.
13. Ibid.
14. John Baillie quoted in *Humanism, Another Battle Line,* ed. William P. King (Nashville: Cokesbury Press, 1931), p. 266; cf. pp. 272ff.
15. Julian S. Huxley, ed., *The Humanist Frame* (New York: Harper & Row, 1961), p. 42. Used by permission.
16. Ibid.
17. Hepburn, "Critique of Humanist Theology," p. 34.
18. S. Radhakrishnan, *An Idealist View of Life* (London: George Allen & Unwin, Ltd., 1933), pp. 69, 56. Used by permission of Barnes & Noble.
19. Bertrand Russell, *Mysticism and Logic and Other Essays* (London: Longmans, 1918), p. 48. Used by permission of George Allen & Unwin, Ltd.
20. D. Elton Trueblood, *Philosophy of Religion* (New York: Harper & Row, 1957), p. 46. Used by permission.
21. Eugene William Lyman, *The Meaning and Truth of Religion* (New York: Charles Scribner's Sons, 1933), p. 191.
22. Blackham, *Objections to Humanism,* p. 16.
23. Ibid., p. 18.
24. Ibid., p. 19.
25. Hepburn, "Critique of Humanist Theology," pp. 48-49.
26. Ibid., p. 49.
27. Radhakrishnan, *An Idealist View of Life,* p. 63.
28. A. E. Taylor, *The Faith of a Moralist* (New York: Macmillan, 1930), pp. 61-62. Used by permission.

29. Alan Richardson, *Science, History and Faith* (New York: Oxford University Press, 1950), pp. 151-52. Used by permission of the author.
30. Rufus Jones, *The Luminous Trail* (New York: Macmillan, 1947), p. 147-48. Copyright 1947 by The Macmillan Company. Used by permission.
31. Ernst Haeckel, *The Riddle of the Universe* (New York: Harper & Bros., 1900), pp. 13-14.
32. Bertrand Russell, "A Free Man's Worship," from *The Basic Writings of Bertrand Russell,* ed. Robert E. Egner and Lester E. Denonn (New York: Simon & Schuster, 1961), p. 67. Copyright © 1961 by George Allen & Unwin, Ltd. Used by permission.
33. Lamont, *The Philosophy of Humanism,* p. 13.
34. Erich Fromm, "The Sane Society," reprinted in *The Nature of Man* by Fromm and Ramon Xirau (New York: Macmillan, 1968), p. 311.
35. From *Living Issues in Philosophy* by Harold H. Titus, p. 218, © 1970 by Litton Educational Publishing, Inc. Reprinted by permission of Van Nostrand Reinhold Company.
36. Ibid.
37. Reinhold Niebuhr, *The Nature and Destiny of Man* (New York: Charles Scribner's Sons, 1941), p. 124. Used by permission.
38. Rufus Jones, *The Testimony of the Soul* (New York: Macmillan, 1936), pp. 63f.
39. Jones, *The Luminous Trail,* pp. 148f.
40. Quoted in *Religious Belief and Philosophical Thought,* ed. William P. Alston (New York: Harcourt, Brace & World, 1963), p. 514.
41. Taylor, *The Faith of a Moralist,* p. 65.
42. Marty, *Varieties of Unbelief,* p. 44.
43. Charles West, *The Power to Be Human* (New York: Macmillan, 1971), p. 35.
44. Gerhard Uhlhorn, *Christian Charity in the Ancient Church* (New York: Charles Scribner's Sons, 1883).
45. Jacques Maritain, *Integral Humanism* (New York: Charles Scribner's Sons, 1968), pp. 4-5. Used by permission.
46. Ibid., p. 6.

5 The Transcendence of Humanism

1. Arthur J. Balfour, *Theism and Humanism* (London: Hodder & Stoughton, 1915), pp. 249-50. Used by permission of the Estate of the late Earl of Balfour.
2. See pp. 36-39 for a summary of the "Manifesto."
3. John H. Dietrich, *The Humanist,* 1953, 13:137. Used by permission.
4. Statement by Jacob J. Weinstein. This article first appeared in *The Humanist,* Mar.-Apr. 1953, p. 70 and is reprinted by permission.
5. A. E. Taylor, *Does God Exist?* (London: Macmillan, 1947), p. v. Used by permission of Macmillan, London and Basingstoke.
6. Balfour, *Theism and Humanism,* p. 23.
7. Ibid., p. 22.
8. Taylor, *Does God Exist?,* p. 34.
9. Ibid., p. 14.
10. Robert Calhoun, *God and the Common Life* (New York: Charles Scribner's Sons, 1935), p. 174. Used by permission.
11. Alfred N. Whitehead, *Science and the Modern World* (New York: Macmillan, 1925), p. 257.
12. John Baillie, *Our Knowledge of God* (New York: Charles Scribner's Sons, 1959), p. 147. Used by permission.
13. Francis McConnell, et al., *Ventures in Belief* (New York: Charles Scribner's Sons, 1930), p. 31.
14. Roger Hazelton, *On Proving God* (New York: Harper & Bros., 1952), p. 59.
15. D. Elton Trueblood, *Philosophy of Religion* (New York: Harper & Row, 1957), pp. 87-88. Used by permission.
16. Ibid., p. 89.
17. E. O. James, *Concept of Deity* (London: Hutchinson's University Library, 1950), p. 130.
18. Ibid.
19. A. E. Taylor, "Theism," *Encyclopedia of Religion and Ethics* (New York: Charles Scribner's Sons, 1955), 12:261.
20. Douglas Macintosh, *My Idea of God,* ed. J. F. Newton (Boston: Little, Brown and Co., 1927), p. 138.
21. Baillie, *Our Knowledge of God,* p. 147.
22. Ibid., pp. 147-48.

23. Ibid., p. 148.
24. William E. Hocking, *Types of Philosophy,* rev. ed. (New York: Charles Scribner's Sons, 1939), p. 442.
25. Georgia Harkness, *Recovery of Ideals* (New York: Charles Scribner's Sons, 1937), p. 100.
26. Calhoun, *God and the Common Life,* p. 178.
27. John Stuart Mill, *Three Essays on Religion: Theism,* pp. 169-70, in George P. Fisher, *Grounds of Theistic and Christian Belief* (New York: Charles Scribner's Sons, 1927), p. 32.
28. William H. Davis, *Philosophy of Religion* (Abilene, Tex.: Biblical Research Press, 1969), p. 17.
29. Reprinted by permission of the New York University Press from *Religious Experience and Truth,* edited by Sidney Hook, p. 213. Copyright © 1961 by New York University.
30. Ibid., p. 218.
31. Fisher, *Grounds of Theistic and Christian Belief,* p. 26.
32. Josiah Royce, *The Spirit of Modern Philosophy* (Boston: Houghton Mifflin Co., 1967), p. 133.
33. Trueblood, *Philosophy of Religion,* p. 112.
34. Peter Bertocci, *Introduction to the Philosophy of Religion* (Englewood Cliffs, N.J.: Prentice-Hall, 1951-58), p. 292. Used by permission of the author.
35. Ibid.
36. Ibid., p. 293.
37. Trueblood, *Philosophy of Religion,* p. 113.
38. Bertocci, *Introduction to the Philosophy of Religion,* p. 299.
39. John C. Bennett, *Christianity and Our World* (New York: Association Press, 1936), p. 7.
40. Lynn H. Hough, *The Christian Criticism of Life* (Nashville: Abingdon-Cokesbury Press, 1941), p. 191. Used by permission.
41. Cf. Rufus Jones, *Social Law in the Spiritual World* (Philadelphia: John C. Winston Company, 1904), pp. 30-37.
42. Harris Franklin Rall, *Christianity* (New York: Charles Scribner's Sons, 1940), pp. 116-17. Used by permission.
43. Burnett H. Streeter, *Reality* (New York: Macmillan, 1926), pp. 137-38. Used by permission.
44. Shailer Mathews, in *Humanism, Another Battle Line,* ed. William King (Nashville: Cokesbury Press, 1931), p. 147.

45. Donald Walhout, *Interpreting Religion* (Englewood Cliffs, N.J.: Prentice-Hall, 1963), p. 191. © 1963 Prentice-Hall, Inc. Used by permission.
46. Taylor, *Does God Exist?*, p. vii.
47. Rall, *Christianity*, pp. 307-8.
48. Ibid., p. 156.
49. Rufus Jones, *A Call to What Is Vital* (New York: Macmillan, 1948), pp. 106-7.
50. From *Living Issues in Philosophy* by Harold H. Titus, p. 443. © 1970 by Litton Educational Publishing Inc. Reprinted by permission of Van Nostrand Reinhold Company.
51. William Temple, *Nature, Man, and God* (New York: St. Martin's Press, 1934, 1960), p. 316. Used by permission of Macmillan, London and Basingstoke.
52. Martin Buber, *A Believing Humanism* (New York: Simon & Schuster, 1967), p. 126. Copyright © 1967 by Maurice Friedman.
53. Temple, *Nature, Man and God*, pp. 323-24.
54. Ibid., p. 324.

6 In Conclusion

1. Irving Babbitt, *Democracy and Leadership* (Boston: Houghton Mifflin Co., 1924), p. 22.
2. George A. Gordon, *New Epoch for Faith* (Boston: Houghton Mifflin Co., 1901), p. 9. Used by permission.
3. S. Paul Schilling, *God in an Age of Atheism* (Nashville: Abingdon Press, 1969), p. 80. Used by permission.
4. Ibid., p. 126.
5. D. Gareth Jones, "The Fragility of Humanism," *Christianity Today,* Aug. 25, 1972, p. 13.
6. Attributed to Karl Groos, *The Problem of Relativism* (n.d.).
7. Francis McConnell, et al., *Ventures in Belief* (New York: Charles Scribner's Sons, 1930), p. 27.
8. Julian S. Huxley, *Religion Without Revelation* (New York: New American Library, 1959), p. 97. Used by permission.
9. Ibid., p. 98.
10. Rufus Jones, *Social Law in the Spiritual World* (Philadelphia: John C. Winston Company, 1904), p. 30.
11. From *Man Without God,* by John Reid, The Westminster

Press, p. 92. Copyright © 1971 Corpus Instrumentorum, Inc. Used by permission.

12. Ibid., p. 86.
13. Gary Schouberg in *The Catholic World,* Nov. 1968. Used by permission.
14. Reid, *Man Without God,* p. 81.
15. See Kingsley Martin's chapter in *Objections to Humanism,* ed. H. J. Blackham (Philadelphia: Lippincott, 1965), p. 83.
16. Reid, *Man Without God,* p. 72.
17. D. Gareth Jones, "Fragility of Humanism," p. 13.
18. Leslie Weatherhead, *The Christian Agnostic* (Nashville: Abingdon Press, 1965), p. 330.
19. Cf. Georgia Harkness, *The Modern Rival of Christian Faith* (Nashville: Abingdon Press, 1952), p. 83.
20. D. Elton Trueblood, *The Life We Prize* (New York: Harper & Row, 1951), p. 112.
21. Arthur James Balfour, *Theism and Humanism* (London: Hodder & Stoughton, 1915), pp. 273-74. Used by permission of the Estate of the late Earl of Balfour.
22. Daniel Callahan, ed., *The Secular City Debate* (New York: Macmillan, 1969), p. 99.
23. The problem of evil is perhaps the most serious challenge to theistic faith. The substance of the problem is that if God is all good and all powerful, he must certainly will the destruction of evil. If it is in his power to do so, why does evil continue? Theists offer a number of tentative solutions to the problem: (1) Much evil is caused by men, and God does not choose to violate man's freedom. (2) Evil is the price we pay for living in an orderly world. (3) This is the best of all possible worlds. (4) There is redemptive value in suffering. (5) Accept it with a childlike faith. For another approach one might examine the solutions suggested by Leslie Weatherhead, *The Will of God* (Nashville: Abingdon-Cokesbury Press, 1945), or C. S. Lewis, *The Problem of Pain* (New York: Macmillan, 1944).
24. Gordon, *New Epoch for Faith,* p. 10.
25. Georgia Harkness, *Stability Amid Change* (Nashville: Abingdon Press, 1969), p. 109; quotations from *The Living Bible,* Exodus 20:13-16.

26. Donald Walhout, *Interpreting Religion* (Englewood Cliffs, N.J.: Prentice-Hall, 1963), p. 191. © 1963 Prentice-Hall, Inc. Used by permission.

27. Arthur James Balfour, *Theism and Humanism* (London: Hodder & Stoughton, 1915). Used by permission of the Estate of the late Earl of Balfour. See John Buchan, *The Pilgrim's Way* (Cambridge: Houghton Mifflin Co., 1940), p. 158.

28. Edgar Brightman, *Religious Values* (Nashville: Abingdon Press, 1925), p. 139.

29. *Time,* Sept. 14, 1970, p. 34.

BIBLIOGRAPHY

Alston, William P. (ed.). *Religious Belief and Philosophical Thought.* New York: Harcourt, Brace & World, 1963.

Baillie, John. *Our Knowledge of God.* New York: Charles Scribner's Sons, 1959.

Balfour, Arthur James. *Foundations of Belief.* New York: Longmans, Green and Co., 1918.

_____. *Theism and Humanism.* London: Hodder & Stoughton, 1915.

Bennett, John C. *Christianity and Our World.* New York: Association Press, 1936.

Bertocci, Peter. *Introduction to the Philosophy of Religion.* Englewood Cliffs, N.J.: Prentice-Hall, 1951-58.

Blackham, H. J. (ed.). *Objections to Humanism.* Philadelphia: J. B. Lippincott, 1965.

Brightman, Edgar S. *Religious Values.* Nashville: Abingdon Press, 1925.

Brinton, Crane. *Ideas and Men.* Englewood Cliffs, N.J.: Prentice-Hall, 1950.

Buber, Martin. *A Believing Humanism.* New York: Simon & Schuster, 1967.

Buchan, John (Lord Tweedsmuir). *The Pilgrim's Way.* Cambridge: Houghton Mifflin Co., 1940.

Calhoun, Robert. *God and the Common Life.* New York: Charles Scribner's Sons, 1935.

Callahan, Daniel (ed.). *The Secular City Debate.* New York: Macmillan, 1969.

Coates, William A., and White, Hayden V. *The Ordeal of Liberal Humanism.* Vol. 2. New York: McGraw-Hill, 1970.

Cox, Harvey. *The Secular City.* New York: Macmillan, 1965.

Dakin, Arthur Hazard. *Man, the Measure.* Princeton: Princeton University Press, 1939.

D'Arcy, Martin C. *Humanism and Christianity.* New York: World Publishing Co., 1969.

Davis, William H. *Philosophy of Religion.* Abilene, Tex.: Biblical Research Press, 1969.

Dewey, John. *A Common Faith.* New Haven, Conn.: Yale University Press, 1934.

Fisher, George P. *Grounds of Theistic and Christian Belief.* New York: Charles Scribner's Sons, 1927.

Fromm, Erich. *Man for Himself.* New York: Holt, Rinehart & Winston, 1947.

Fromm, Erich and Xirau, Ramon. *The Nature of Man.* New York: Macmillan, 1968.

Gordon, George A. *New Epoch for Faith.* Boston: Houghton Mifflin Co., 1901.

Hackman, George, Kegley, Charles, and Nikander, Viljo. *Religion in Modern Life.* New York: Macmillan, 1957.

Haeckel, Ernst. *The Riddle of the Universe.* New York: Harper & Row, 1900.

Harkness, Georgia. *The Modern Rival of Christian Faith.* Nashville: Abingdon Press, 1952.

_____. *Recovery of Ideals.* New York: Charles Scribner's Sons, 1937.

_____. *Stability Amid Change.* Nashville: Abingdon Press, 1969.

Hazelton, Roger. *On Proving God.* New York: Harper & Bros., 1952.

Hocking, William E. *Types of Philosophy.* Rev. ed. New York: Charles Scribner's Sons, 1939.

Hook, Sidney (ed.). *Religious Experience and Truth.* New York: New York University Press, 1961.

Hough, Lynn H. *The Christian Criticism of Life.* Nashville: Abingdon-Cokesbury Press, 1941.

The Humanist. Vol. 13, 1953.

Hutchinson, John and Martin, James A. *Ways of Faith.* 2d ed. New York: Ronald Press, 1960.

Huxley, Julian S. *Religion Without Revelation.* New York: New American Library, 1959.

Huxley, Julian S. (ed.). *The Humanist Frame.* New York: Harper & Row, 1961.

James, E. O. *Concept of Deity.* London: Hutchinson's University Library, 1950.

Jaspers, Karl. *Man in the Modern Age.* New York: Doubleday, 1957.

Jones, Rufus. *A Call to What Is Vital.* New York: Macmillan, 1948.

_____. *The Luminous Trail.* New York: Macmillan, 1947.

_____. *Social Law in the Spiritual World.* Philadelphia: John C. Winston Company, 1904.

_____. *The Testimony of the Soul.* New York: Macmillan, 1936.

King, William (ed.). *Humanism, Another Battle Line.* Nashville: Cokesbury Press, 1931.

Kitwood, T. M. *What Is Human?* London: Inter-Varsity Press, 1970.

Lamont, Corliss. *The Philosophy of Humanism.* New York: Frederick Ungar Publishing Co., 1949, 1965.

Levi, Albert William. *Humanism and Politics.* Bloomington, Ind.: Indiana University Press, 1969.

Lippmann, Walter. *The Public Philosophy.* New York: New American Library, 1955.

Lyman, Eugene William. *The Meaning and Truth of Religion.* New York: Charles Scribner's Sons, 1933.

Macintosh, Douglas. *My Idea of God.* Ed. J. F. Newton. Boston: Little, Brown and Co., 1927.

Malone, David. "Bertrand Russell's Concept of the Basis of Ethical Value." An unpublished thesis, Abilene Christian College, 1963.

Maritain, Jacques. *Integral Humanism.* New York: Charles Scribner's Sons, 1968.

Marty, Martin. *Varieties of Unbelief.* New York: Doubleday, 1964.

McConnell, Francis, et al. *Ventures in Belief.* New York: Charles Scribner's Sons, 1930.

Munson, Gorham. *The Dilemma of the Liberated.* New York: Coward-McCann, 1930.

The New Humanist. May-June, 1933.

Newton, Joseph Fort (ed.). *My Idea of God.* Boston: Little, Brown and Co., 1927.

Niebuhr, Reinhold. *The Nature and Destiny of Man.* New York: Charles Scribner's Sons, 1941, 1943.

Novak, Michael. *Belief and Unbelief.* New York: New American Library, 1965.

Otto, Max C. *Things and Ideals.* New York: Henry Holt & Co., 1924.

Radhakrishnan, S. *An Idealist View of Life.* London: George Allen and Unwin, 1933, 1937.

Rall, Harris Franklin. *Christianity.* New York: Charles Scribner's Sons, 1940.

Reid, John. *Man Without God.* Philadelphia: Westminster Press, 1971.

Richardson, Alan. *Science, History and Faith.* New York: Oxford University Press, 1950, 1960.

Royce, Josiah. *The Spirit of Modern Philosophy.* Boston: Houghton Mifflin Co., 1967.

Russell, Bertrand. "A Free Man's Worship," *Basic Writings of Bertrand Russell,* ed. Robert E. Egner and Lester E. Denonn. New York: Simon & Schuster, 1961.

_____. "What I Believe." *The Nation,* 133, Apr. 29, 1931.

Schilling, S. Paul. *God in an Age of Atheism.* Nashville: Abingdon Press, 1969.

Schilpp, Paul Arthur (ed.). *The Philosophy of Bertrand Russell.* Evanston, Ill.: Northwestern University Press, 1944.

Sorley, W. R. *Moral Values and the Idea of God.* New York: Cambridge University Press, 1918.

Streeter, Burnett H. *Reality.* New York: Macmillan, 1926.

Taylor, A. E. *Does God Exist?* New York: Macmillan, 1947.

_____. *The Faith of a Moralist.* New York: Macmillan, 1930.

_____. "Theism." *Encyclopedia of Religion and Ethics.* Ed. James Hastings. New York: Charles Scribner's Sons, 1955.

Temple, William. *Nature, Man and God.* New York: Macmillan, 1934, 1960.

Tillich, Paul. *The Protestant Era.* Chicago: University of Chicago Press, 1948.

Titus, Harold H. *Living Issues in Philosophy.* New York: D. Van Nostrand Co., 1970.

Trueblood, D. Elton. *The Life We Prize.* New York: Harper & Row, 1951.

_____. *Philosophy of Religion.* New York: Harper & Row, 1957.

Uhlhorn, Gerhard. *Christian Charity in the Ancient Church.* New York: Charles Scribner's Sons, 1883.

Walhout, Donald. *Interpreting Religion.* Englewood Cliffs, N.J.: Prentice-Hall, 1963.

Weatherhead, Leslie. *The Christian Agnostic.* Nashville: Abingdon Press, 1965.

West, Charles. *The Power to Be Human.* New York: Macmillan, 1971.

Whitehead, Alfred N. *Science and the Modern World.* New York: Macmillan, 1925.

Wieman, Henry N. *American Philosophies of Religion.* New York: Harper & Row, 1936.

Wyckoff, Robert S. and Bowers, Frederick A. (eds.). *Contemporary Religious Thinking.* New York: Falcon Press, 1933.